About the Authors

The authors discovered a shared interest in marriage, adultery, bigamy and divorce (purely from an academic perspective!) over breakfast at a conference. As the story of Henry Cecil's life and loves unites all these elements, they decided to join forces and use their expertise to untangle the drama that unfolded in Hanbury Hall, Burghley House, and the village of Great Bolas in the late eighteenth century.

Dr Julie Shaffer's work has focused on women novelists of the Romantic era and the British novel in the 18th and 19th centuries, and she has written on the scandalous lives of such female authors as Mary Robinson, whose lovers included Prince George; Professor Rebecca Probert has written widely on the laws relating to marriage and cohabitation since 1600, a subject on which she is a leading authority; and Dr Joanne Bailey is an expert on the history of the family and marriage in Britain and is the author of numerous books and articles on married women and the law. Rebecca and Joanne have appeared on BBC TV's *Who Do You Think You Are?* and on a number of TV and radio programmes talking about the history of marriage and family life. It was one of these—*Great Houses*, with Julian Fellowes—that sparked their interest in Henry's story.

Professor Rebecca Probert is Professor of Law at the University of Warwick; Dr Julie Shaffer is Professor in English at the University of Wisconsin Oshkosh; and Dr Joanne Bailey is a Reader in History at Oxford Brookes University.

The West elevation of Burghley House in 1755

a noble affair

the remarkable true story of the runaway wife, the bigamous earl, and the farmer's daughter

BRANDRAM

2013

First published in Great Britain in 2013
by Brandram, an imprint of Takeaway (Publishing)

1st edition, 1.0

Takeaway (Publishing), 33 New Street, Kenilworth CV8 2EY

E-mail: books@takeawaypublishing.co.uk

British Library Cataloguing in Publication Data.
A catalogue record for this book is available from the British Library

ISBN 978-0-9563847-8-2

Contents

Introduction

A Country Wedding

On April 13th, 1790, a simple country wedding took place in the Shropshire village of Great Bolas. The bride, Sarah Hoggins, had been born in the parish and was a familiar figure there. Just a few months short of her seventeenth birthday, she was the eldest daughter of a local farmer, Thomas Hoggins.

The groom, by contrast, had arrived in Great Bolas only the previous year under somewhat mysterious circumstances. The fact that he received sums of money at irregular intervals did lead some villagers to wonder exactly who or what he was. Some apparently thought that he must be a highwayman, since this would also explain his sporadic and unexplained absences from the village.

He signed his name in the marriage register as John Jones—which was indeed the name by which he was known in the little community. But it was not the name with which he had been baptised. 'John Jones' was in fact 36-year-old Henry Cecil, heir-presumptive to the Earl of Exeter. And he was already married.

The story of Henry Cecil and his matrimonial entanglements is one that has been told in poetry, song, ballet, and (often purple) prose. Nineteenth-century accounts glossed over some of the less flattering details; twentieth-century accounts, by contrast, revelled in them. How each retelling has reflected the preoccupations of its own time is a story in its own right, as the final chapter will show. But there are three key accounts that merit a mention at this early stage, both to highlight some of the difficulties that we have encountered in researching this story and how this new book differs from them.

The Cottage Countess, Sydney Watson's 'historical romance' on the story, published in 1974, takes the bare bones and weaves an enjoyable but inevitably invented dialogue between the main characters. A second book, Elizabeth Inglis-Jones' avowedly 'essentially truthful narrative' *The Lord of Burghley*, published in 1964, is equally entertaining, if equally speculative on certain points. Of a very different nature though is Andrew Harris' meticulously researched work, *The Vernons of Hanbury*.[1] This is an in-depth study of the family of Henry's first wife, Emma Vernon, with two chapters being devoted to their marriage and its aftermath. It is far more accurate than earlier accounts, since Harris was able for the first time to draw on Henry's correspondence with his friend the Reverend Burslem, which completely undermined some of the myths that had grown up around the story. We are very grateful to Andrew Harris for making his work available to us, and for his generosity in discussing various aspects of the story.

Our retelling has not ventured beyond the known facts of the story (although we do mention some of the speculations of earlier authors and hope that readers will enjoy the amusing discrepancies that we highlight). As scholars with a particular interest in marriage and divorce in the late eighteenth century, we have instead sought to illuminate the story by setting it in the context of its age. While no other case quite matches that of Henry, Emma and Sarah in terms of its drama, the stories of other bigamists and divorcing couples of the time can tell us far more about what our three main protagonists were going through than any imagined conversations. As is often the case, the truth turns out to be stranger—and more interesting—than fiction.

chapter 1

The Heir to an Earldom

On a December night in 1754, an unlikely group of persons arrived at a house in Canterbury after crossing the English Channel. There was a Belgian doctor named Van der Belen, a London attorney named Robert Barber, a Flemish wet-nurse, and one or two others. And—most importantly of all—there was a nine-month-old baby, who stood to inherit an earldom and vast wealth. This miscellaneous group of people had been assembled for the sole purpose of conveying 'little Harry Cecil' from his parents on the Continent to his uncle and aunt at Burghley House, the spectacular Elizabethan building that had been home to successive Earls of Exeter since the start of the seventeenth century.

It sounds like the stuff of fairy tales, and indeed none of those who have chronicled Henry's story, even in their wilder flights of fancy, have dared to imagine such a dramatic beginning. Yet we can be sure of the details, because they are recorded in a brief note by George Aufrère, a wealthy London cloth merchant who was related to the Cecils by marriage and who was present in the house to which baby Henry was brought that night.[1]

But what lay behind this strange transaction? Why was Henry born overseas, and why was he being taken from his parents at such a young age? To understand this we need to delve a little further back into the family history of the Cecils.

As with many aristocratic families, the fortunes of the Cecils had waxed and waned. Burghley House had been built in the late sixteenth century by William Cecil, Secretary of State and later Lord High Treasurer under Queen Elizabeth I, and raised to the peerage as Baron Burghley in 1571. William's eldest son,

Thomas, was created Earl of Exeter under James I in 1605. But it was his younger son, Thomas' half-brother Robert, who carried on William Cecil's political role and influence, having been created Earl of Salisbury on the same day. During the seventeenth century the Earls of Exeter played a relatively minor role in affairs of state, while at the same time managing to get through a considerable amount of money.

By 1700, the Burghley estate was hugely endebted. The sixth Earl died in 1721, and his eldest son the following year. But then, in 1724, the fortunes of the family changed. On July 18th, 1724, the new and eighth Earl of Exeter, Brownlow Cecil, married Hannah Sophia Chambers at the church of St James, Westminster. As the daughter of a Derby merchant, Thomas Chambers, she was not the Earl's match in status. But she brought considerable wealth to the marriage. It was widely reported that her fortune was '£40,000 down'—i.e. paid outright—and 'as much more at the death of the Lady's father.'[2]

As the historian John Cannon has noted, careful marriages 'were of great importance in consolidating or increasing family fortunes.'[3] He gives the example of the other branch of the Cecil family, the Earls of Salisbury, noting that their 'shaky position' was 'restored by the marriage in 1683 to the daughter of Simon Bennet, who had amassed great London wealth.'[4] For some families, increasing wealth led to increased rank—the Grosvenor family, for example, rose from a mere barony in the mid eighteenth century to an earldom, then a marquisate, and eventually, in the late nineteenth century, a dukedom. Others used such monies to enhance their lands and houses.

The most significant changes to Burghley House were not to come until the next generation, and enhanced rank would come a generation after that, but at least the estate was now on a sounder financial footing. In the meantime, Brownlow and Hannah went on to have six children—Brownlow, named after his father, born in 1725, Margaret Sophia in 1726,

Thomas Chambers (named after his maternal grandfather) in 1728, Elizabeth in 1729, Ann in 1734, and David in 1736. Two died before reaching adulthood: the youngest, David, before attaining his first year, and the oldest daughter, Margaret, in 1738. Ann too died unmarried, although she at least attained the age of fifty. Elizabeth was to outlive them all—and we shall meet her again. But for now the focus is on the two eldest sons, who are both central to our story.

Brownlow Cecil followed the usual path of an elder son: after attending Winchester School and St John's College, Cambridge, he was elected to the House of Commons for the County of Rutland in 1747, while still only twenty-one.[5] At the age of twenty-four he made a suitable match to Letitia Townshend, grand-daughter of Sir Horatio Townshend, 1st Viscount Townshend, and the only daughter and (according to the marriage settlement) co-heiress of the Hon. Horatio Townshend.[6]

But while Brownlow became an MP and married well, his younger brother Thomas followed a rather different course. He has been (not entirely unfairly) dismissed as 'a weak and undistinguished character about whose wasted life practically nothing is known.'[7] We know that, like many younger sons, he went into the army, a commission with the Coldstream Regiment of the Foot Guards having been purchased for him. He was not, however, destined to make a career as a soldier, for in 1751 it was reported that 'The Hon. Mr Cecil, Son of the Earl of Exeter, upon some Disgust, lately resigned his commission in the Foot Guards, and on Monday last set out for the Court of France.'[8]

With Thomas, we can assume, went his new wife. In February of 1751 Thomas had married Charlotte Garnier, a dancer, said to be of Basque extraction.[9] This was hardly a good match even for an impoverished younger son. It was also celebrated clandestinely. The wedding took place at the May Fair chapel in London, one of the places to which couples resorted when they wished to marry secretly and speedily.[10]

Just how speedily couples could marry there is illustrated by a union that took place just a year later, on Valentine's Day in 1752, when the sixth Duke of Hamilton met and married the beautiful Elizabeth Gunning, although there may be some poetic licence in the suggestion that this occurred in 'whirlwind style at midnight… with a curtain ring'.[11]

At the time, it should be noted, a marriage was still perfectly valid even if it was celebrated 'clandestinely'—without either banns being called in church or a licence having been obtained. All that was strictly necessary was for the marriage to be celebrated by an Anglican clergyman, and the *bona fide* credentials of those who married couples at the May Fair chapel were well advertised.[12] But such clandestine marriages were regarded with disfavour, especially by the families whose offspring entered into *mésalliances* as a result. Only two years after Thomas and Charlotte's wedding, legislation was passed to shut down the trade in clandestine marriages.[13]

It is safe to infer that Thomas' marriage to a dancing girl was not a match that had the approval or countenance of his family. Such social mismatches were, though, relatively rare. While there were a number of memorable examples, most were 'the product of the impetuosity of youth, the complaisance of age or the delay of faculties' and 'certainly do not mean that there was not a very powerful prejudice against marrying outside one's order'.[14] As the clergyman Henry Stebbing wrote a few years after Thomas's wedding, 'the world *naturally* runs this way without the help of laws. The lower classes of men have it not in their *power* to marry above their rank, or very rarely. The rich and great have as rarely so little *pride* as to permit them to marry below theirs.'[15]

Over half a century later, Jane Austen has Colonel Fitzwilliam somewhat plaintively tell Elizabeth Bennett in *Pride and Prejudice* that the younger sons of an earl 'cannot marry where they like…. Our habits of life make us too dependent, and there are not many in my rank of life who can afford to marry without some attention to money.'[16]

In Thomas' case, the result of his imprudent marriage to Charlotte was a lifetime of debt. In a letter, Thomas was later to acknowledge that he had 'left England in conformity to the desires of my Brother, and the rest of my friends.'[17] A note of pique is evident in his adding that he would have been very happy to oblige them by remaining out of the country, and complaining that Brownlow had not sorted out the financial problems caused by his 'former indiscretions and extravagences.' Thomas, in short, comes across as someone who expected his older brother to pay for his mistakes, and petulant into the bargain.

But Thomas was luckier than his older brother in one respect, for he had fathered a son. In November of 1754 it was recorded in Brussels that a child of Lieutenant Thomas Chambers Cecil was said to have been born at the house of a wine merchant, known as the sign of the Swan, some eight months previously.

While Henry's birthplace was a long way from the Elizabethan splendour of Burghley House in every respect, things were about to change—as, indeed, was reflected by the fact that Henry's birth was only belatedly being recorded. For on November 3rd, 1754, Thomas' father, the 8th Earl of Exeter, had died. The subsequent swift sequence of events—the record of Henry's birth being made on November 23rd and his being conveyed to England in early December—suggests that little time was wasted in informing Thomas of the death of the eighth Earl and the wish of his successor, Thomas' elder brother Brownlow, to have baby Henry brought to Burghley.

Technically, of course, it was Thomas himself who was next in line to the earldom after his brother Brownlow, and it was far from unknown for estates and titles to pass to a younger sibling when their elder brother died without issue. Thomas and Brownlow's own grandfather had inherited Burghley in this way. Even so, there seems to have been no invitation to Thomas to return to England.

And it is telling that, in George Aufrère's account of the events of December 10th and Henry's arrival in England, there is no mention of Thomas being present. This might have been tactful: Aufrère was writing for the benefit of the new Earl, who may not have welcomed the news that his younger brother had returned to England, even if only for the purpose of bringing Henry across the Channel. But we know that Thomas was there from another document in the Burghley archives. Dated the day after Henry's arrival in Canterbury, Wednesday, December 11th, Thomas Chambers Cecil certified that he had delivered 'his only child Henry, aged about nine months' to his brother's London attorney, Robert Barber, 'to convey to my mother, the Countess of Exeter.' Another memorandum, signed by those present, reported that it was Thomas who delivered Henry 'into the hands of George Aufrère... by Lady Exeter's order.' Thomas also certified that the child had been 'lawfully begotten by him on the body of his wife Charlotte.' This was an essential detail. Had Henry been born illegitimate he would have had no entitlement to inherit either the title or the estate.

There was, of course, one other event that might have led to baby Henry losing his place in the succession. If Brownlow were to have a son, then he, not Henry, would follow in his father's footsteps as Earl of Exeter. This means that the timing of events suddenly looks rather more puzzling. By 1754 Brownlow had been married for around five years, and both he and his wife Letitia were only in their late twenties. That he acted so swiftly *after* his father's death might suggest that he was aware that he was unlikely to have any children of his own to succeed him. That he waited *until* his father's death might also suggest that this was not something that he wished to admit to his sire.

What we do know is that Brownlow's marriage to Letitia did indeed prove childless, as she died after a brief illness at the relatively young age of thirty, when Henry was just two years old. Of course, Brownlow was still relatively young,

Henry's uncle, Brownlow Cecil, 9th Earl of Exeter

and there was every likelihood of him marrying again and having a son to succeed him. Nonetheless, for the time being Henry was the only child of the next generation, and had to be educated as befitted the rank he might one day fill. Sent to Eton at the age of ten, he also had a private tutor, one Mr Weston, and spent his holidays at Burghley House.

Some of those who have chronicled Henry's story have assumed that his relationship with his uncle Brownlow was cold and distant. Indeed, the nineteenth-century writer Edward Walford seems blithely unaware of Brownlow's role in Henry's upbringing, claiming that 'no love was lost between them' and that 'while the old earl lived the young man kept pretty clear of Burleigh and all its belongings.'[18] But Henry's later letters suggest that Brownlow was one of the most important people in his life. Their relationship may well have had its difficulties—Brownlow has been described as kind but complex—but there was clearly a great deal of affection and regard on both sides.

There is, however, an intriguing puzzle as to what happened next. In April of 1770, just as Henry was approaching his sixteenth birthday, the *London Evening Post* reported that Brownlow had at last remarried:

> On Monday night, and not sooner, was married at Burleigh, by the Rev Mr Digby, the Right Hon the Earl of Exeter, to Miss Anna Maria Cheatham, youngest daughter of the late Job Cheatham Esq, of Sodor-Hall near Beverley in the county of York.[19]

The news was taken up by a number of other newspapers, and Anna Maria Cecil, née Cheatham, found her way into standard lists of the British peerage. Henry's biographers have seen his uncle's remarriage, and the increased likelihood of his producing an heir, as a severe blow to the young man, and have assumed that the consequent uncertainty over his future status may well have had an impact on Henry's psychological make-up. One even talks of 'an icy wind that threatened to ruin his prospects which had seemed to be so secure and which for years he had been encouraged to believe in. Now a host of nagging uncertainties gnawed at the very foundations of his life. Position, possessions, everything he relied on were slipping from his grasp....'[20]

If Henry's uncle Brownlow *had* remarried and in time fathered an heir, this might well have been the case. But there is a large question mark over whether his uncle's marriage to 'Miss Cheatham' ever actually happened. For a start, there is no record of it in the parish register for Stamford, the town situated just a mile from Burghley. As an Earl, Brownlow could of course have obtained a special licence to have the marriage celebrated more privately at Burghley House. Though the law had, since 1754, required all marriages to take place in a church, the Archbishop of Canterbury still had the power to grant special licences to enable a marriage to be celebrated at any time or place. While the availability of such licences was limited to 'Peers, and Peeresses in their own right of Great Britain and Ireland, to their sons and daughters, to Dowager Peeresses, to Privy Councillors, to Judges of his Majesty's Courts in Westminster Hall, to Baronets and Knights and to members of the House of Commons', Brownlow most certainly fell within this select group. Had the marriage been celebrated in this way it would not necessarily have been recorded in any local register. But there is no indication of any such licence having been granted.

Another significant absence is the lack of any marriage settlement. When Brownlow had married Letitia back in 1748, there had, as was usual within aristocratic families, been a detailed marriage settlement indicating what money she was to receive in the event of his demise and vice versa. No such document exists in relation to the mysterious Anna Maria Cheatham.

Not only is there no record of the marriage, there is no record of the bride. No picture of her exists at Burghley House. No record has been traced of her baptism, or of that of her supposed father Job. And no record exists of her death. Of course, given that parish registers from this time were not always carefully kept, as well as the inevitable loss of records over the intervening centuries, a failure to trace a particular event can never be regarded as proof that it did not take place. Nor can a failure to trace a particular person automatically be taken as evidence that no such individual existed. But when thorough searches in gazetteers of the day for the supposed family house of 'Sodor-Hall' also prove fruitless, then one has to ask whether the initial story of the wedding in the *London Evening Post* was in fact true.

And the *Morning Chronicle* of September 20th, 1773, has a letter which indicates that it was not:

> Sir, Your correspondent *Vericola's* remark upon the compiler of the Annual Register's veracity is just, and the doer of it deserves a severe reprimand; I would beg leave to ask the compiler of it… where he got the following piece of authentic intelligence, which in the succeeding volumes stands still uncorrected. In the catalogue of marriages in the year 1770, April 23, we read—"The Earl of Exeter married to Miss Anna Maria Cheatham, of Soderhall, Yorkshire"—If the Annual Register is to be regarded as a Chronicle of Events, the facts should be well authenticated; - whereas the above paragraph could only appear as a piece of low wit in a common News-paper, and a banter upon the noble Earl. *Vericola Seconda.*

So here we have an explicit claim that the original announcement of Brownlow's remarriage was a complete fabrication—a prank. This would explain the absence of any record of either it or Anna Maria. Precisely why someone thought that it would be amusing to publish such a story must remain a matter of speculation: was it perhaps an allusion to some illicit relationship? For the modern reader, 'Sodor-Hall' might sound like 'sod all', as though the woman in question had nothing to bring to the union, but this phrase had not yet been coined. Was it, perhaps, a bantering reference to sodomy? The Burghley archives contain information about an annuity of £200 that was being paid in 1777 to a certain *James* Cheatham—no insignificant sum—but nothing more on the reason why, or on who James was.[21] Or was the 'Anna Maria' a none-too-subtle reference to the artist Angelica Kauffman—born Anna Maria Angelica Catharina Kauffman—whom Brownlow idolised, buying fourteen of her paintings, and who was on occasion a guest at Burghley House? Did the prankster wish to imply a relationship between Angelica and Brownlow?

Regrettably, after the passing of more than two centuries, unless new documents come to light we will most likely never know. But assuming that no such remarriage took place, then this casts a very different light on Henry's upbringing. As long as his uncle remained unmarried, then Henry's chances of succeeding to the earldom were unaffected, his confidence and happiness unimpaired. And with the death of his father Thomas in 1773, Henry was now the next in line after his uncle.[22]

So what was Henry like? Certainly the glimpses of him that we gain through contemporary accounts are ones of a young man of considerable poise. Little is known about his time at St John's College, Cambridge—save that he would have rubbed shoulders there not only with other scions of the nobility but also many men of humbler rank[23]—but we do know that at the age of 20 he was elected as Member of Parliament for Stamford. We know too that he travelled widely in Europe, for in 1775 we find him being presented at court and making something of a hit on account of his knowledge of the Queen's German homeland. The *Gazetteer and New Daily Advertiser* reported that Henry, 'just arrived from making the tour of

Europe', was introduced to Queen Charlotte at St James' by her brother Prince Ernest of Mecklenburgh, and that 'after the Drawing Room was over he held a conversation for upwards of an hour with her Majesty and her brother, he having been at Mecklenburgh, and in great esteem with Her Majesty's brother and sister there.'[24]

A year later Henry was featuring in the columns of newspapers again, as rumours of an impending marriage circulated. The *Middlesex Journal and Evening Advertiser* reported in March of 1776 that 'a treaty of marriage is said to be on foot, and will be solemnised in a few days, between Miss Vernon, of Bond-Street, a lady of a very large fortune, and a yearly estate of £8,000 per annum, and the Hon. Mr Cecil.'[25] And in due course, if a couple of months later than predicted, Henry did indeed marry Emma Vernon at the fashionable church of St George, Hanover Square.

In the meantime, London society had been transfixed by the trial for bigamy of Elizabeth, Duchess of Kingston.[26] Clandestinely (but nevertheless validly) married to an aristocratic young man named Augustus Hervey in 1744, Elizabeth had subsequently obtained what was known as a 'decree of jactitation' from the ecclesiastical court. Technically this was to prevent Augustus from claiming that they were married, although it would appear that he was equally eager to deny the marriage. In 1769, four months after the decree was issued, Elizabeth had married Evelyn Pierrepont, the Duke of Kingston. After his death in 1773, upon which the Duke had left Elizabeth all his property, the Duke's family was keen to show that *his* marriage to Elizabeth had never been valid on account of her previous marriage to Augustus. Tried and convicted of bigamy before the full House of Lords, Elizabeth nonetheless escaped the punishment usually accorded to bigamists—that of branding on the hand—by pleading the 'benefit of peerage'. After all, even though she was no longer technically a Duchess, she was still a Countess, her first husband Augustus having succeeded to the earldom of Bristol a few years earlier. The fact that Elizabeth had in effect got away scot-free with bigamy was a stark reminder of the privileges accorded to people of rank, and the case was so well known at the time that this salient fact must have lodged in Henry's awareness.

At the time of his marriage to Emma Vernon, Henry was twenty-two years of age—relatively young for the late eighteenth century, when most men married in their late twenties. His bride was just a year younger, making them closer in age than was the case for many of their contemporaries, given the trend for aristocratic men to marry later, and their brides to be considerably younger. Emma was, in addition, every bit as wealthy as the *Middlesex Journal and Evening Advertiser* had suggested: her family might not have belonged to the aristocracy, but she was the only child—and sole heiress—of Thomas and Emma Vernon of Hanbury Hall.

Built at the beginning of the eighteenth century by an earlier Thomas Vernon—a successful Chancery lawyer who also served as a Member of Parliament—Hanbury Hall was, and still is, an attractive and substantial red-brick building, filled with beautiful paintings and set amongst the rolling farmland of Worcestershire, a journey of some 100 miles from Burghley across the English midlands. An inventory taken in 1721 recorded that the parlour alone was hung with 102 pictures,[27] while the Great Staircase wound its way past enormous murals painted by Sir James Thornhill, who was subsequently commissioned to decorate both the Painted Hall at Greenwich and the cupola of St Paul's Cathedral. Thomas Vernon, Emma's father, had inherited the hall from his spendthrift father Bowater in 1735, at the age of just 11, but before his death in 1771 had proudly recorded in his will that the estate was clear of debt.

And of course from Emma's point of view the match was an even more prestigious one: by marrying Henry she would, in due course, become Countess of Exeter, and move from the ranks of the gentry to the aristocracy. Hanbury Hall, while impressive, could not hold a candle to the grandeur of Burghley House. So Henry Cecil and Emma Vernon were well matched in terms of age and advantage. And they had something else in common—the fact that both sets of parents had married clandestinely.

The marriage between Emma's parents is surrounded by even more of a mystery than that between Henry's aristocratic father and dancing-girl mother. In 1771 her father Thomas wrote in his will of his 'dear wife' Emma, adding rather intriguingly that he had been 'really married' to her but that this had been 'for some time kept a secret lest it should affect my mother who was then in a bad state of health.'[28] Why Thomas thought his mother would have been so affected by news of his marriage is unclear. The match between Thomas Vernon esquire, Member of Parliament and owner of Hanbury Hall, and Emma Cornwall, the daughter of Vice Admiral Charles Cornwall, was hardly a mismatch. She was, admittedly, somewhat older than him—being aged about forty at the time of their marriage, when he was only twenty-seven—but such age differences could be overlooked if the union was otherwise suitable.

On the face of it, then, the marriage between Emma's parents was far more socially suitable than that between Henry's. Nonetheless it, too, was celebrated clandestinely—that is to say, without observing all of the requirements of the Church's canon law—and apparently in the very same May Fair Chapel where Thomas Cecil and Charlotte had married, possibly even in the same year. The reason why the place and date cannot be stated with any more certainty is that no record of the marriage appears in the register of the chapel, the sole evidence of its location coming from a later letter written to Emma after her marriage to Henry. Although the writer, Dr Thomas Mallié, assured Emma that 'your mother had a very ample certificate from the minister who married them,'[29] this, by itself, would not have been regarded as good evidence of the marriage by any court at the time. The reason for this lay simply in the courts' dislike for the somewhat shady, no-questions-asked practices of such marriage chapels as that of May Fair, whose parsons would willingly join couples in holy matrimony without enquiring whether they were, legally speaking, free and able to marry.

In one contemporary case the court had expressed its suspicion of the evidence put forward, taking the view that it had been fabricated by the parson 'with a view either of producing it... or of suppressing it, as it should appear most advantageous to himself.'[30] In other words, any man willing to officiate at a clandestine marriage was thought to be not above lying in court on behalf of whichever side was willing to pay the most money. Lord Hardwicke, the architect of the Clandestine Marriages Act that stamped out the trade at the May Fair Chapel and the Fleet prison just a few years later, was reputed to have torn up one Fleet register that had been produced in court, refusing to admit it as evidence.[31] Some judges were willing to accept such registers as part of the package of evidence presented to the court, as long as there was other evidence that the marriage had actually taken place, such as the fact that the couple had lived together and been assumed to be husband and wife by friends and family.[32] Others, however, refused to give the registers any credence whatsoever.

So even if the marriage of Emma's parents had been duly entered in the May Fair Chapel register, this would not have been regarded as evidence in the case of any dispute. But the positive absence of any such entry, when combined with Thomas Vernon's determination to keep the marriage a secret from his mother, suggests that the lack of any entry was due to deliberate, rather than accidental, omission. With such duplicitous parsons on hand, one could easily pay for a marriage not to be registered, just as one could pay for a fictitious entry of a marriage to be inserted. The duplicate books kept by those who carried on the trade in clandestine marriages ensured that proof could be produced or not, depending on what money was to be made from either revealing or suppressing the details of a marriage.

Such disreputable behaviour illustrates the lack of security that attended clandestine marriages, and the risks that a woman such as Emma Cornwall was running in marrying in this way. For while there were doubtless advantages to being able to marry swiftly and anonymously in a clandestine ceremony—for a start, parents were unable to object to a social mismatch or an undesirable spouse—there were often tragic downsides: if one partner to the marriage decided to disavow their union, it was all too easy for them to bribe a parson to produce a forged marriage register and deny any knowledge of the ceremony. And there were many examples of one partner discovering only too late that their spouse was in fact already married to another person, rendering their clandestine marriage void and any children bastards.

Perhaps to put paid to any such doubts, Thomas and Emma Vernon subsequently went through a second ceremony of marriage. We might get some idea of why they chose to do this from the words which another eighteenth-century husband used to reassure his wife: 'My dear, don't cry, tho' we were married at the Fleet, I'll marry you again at Church if you desire it.'[33] However, whether Thomas and Emma's second ceremony did actually take place in a church is unclear. Dr Mallié, when writing to Emma in 1780, told her that he had attended this second ceremony on November 23rd, 1754, and that it was 'conducted by a properly licensed clergyman' who 'possessed a living in Oxford or Gloucs or both and was a friend of your fathers.'[34] Before March 25th, 1754, the presence of such an ordained clergyman would have been all that was necessary to create a valid marriage. After that date, by contrast, a marriage had to be preceded either by the calling of banns or the obtaining of a licence, and it had to be celebrated in church, otherwise it was not valid. The only exception to this was if the parties married by a special licence granted by the Archbishop of Canterbury. As an MP, Thomas Vernon would have been entitled to apply for such a licence, which would have allowed the wedding to take place at home, at any time of the day or night. But there is no evidence that he did apply, and the records disclose no such licence having been granted.

Still, given that the first marriage at the May Fair Chapel would have been regarded as valid, the nature of the second ceremony did not actually matter—as long as the union was never challenged. And there would, of course, have been a certain embarrassment in any more public a wedding if Thomas and Emma had been living together as man and wife since the time of that first ceremony. It would seem that this second ceremony was simply intended to act as a reassurance to Emma, then heavily pregnant, rather than to redress any legal problems with the first.

Within a very few weeks of her second marriage ceremony, Emma had given birth to her first child, who was named after her. Baby Emma was born on December 9th, 1754—by coincidence, just as her future husband Henry was being conveyed across the Channel to be handed over to his relations at Burghley House.

Like Henry, Emma was to be an only child. A younger brother, Thomas, was born on May 10th, 1756, but died the same day.[35] And, again like Henry, Emma was to lose her father at a relatively early age. In December of 1771 the list of deaths in the newspapers included a sad announcement:

Last Monday evening at his Seat at Hanbury Hall, in Worcestershire, Thomas Vernon, Esq; formerly one of the Representatives in Parliament for the City of Worcester. He was suddenly struck speechless by a Fit of Apoplexy, while he was out a Hunting that Day, and expired a short Time after he was carried Home.[36]

He was just 47, and he had died on Emma's seventeenth birthday.

Under the terms of Thomas's will—made a few months earlier, which, as has been pointed out, 'must give rise to the suspicion that in the period leading up to his stroke he was not feeling well'[37]—generous provision of £1,600 per year was made for his widow. But the bulk of the estate was held on trust for 'my dear daughter Emma'. She was now an heiress—even if she was to enjoy merely a life interest in the estate, with her father directing that after her death it should pass to her eldest son.

The next glimpse that we have of Emma indicates that she was being 'educated in all the social graces.'[38] While living at the family's London residence in New Bond Street, there were bills for music lessons and dancing lessons.

It is clear that Emma's father had not anticipated her marrying into the peerage. In his will, when setting out the terms of her life interest, he had added that

> I hereby recommend to such Husband or Husbands as my said daughter shall happen to marry… to take upon themselves respectively the surname of Vernon and to use the same and the arms of Vernon.[39]

A similar recommendation was made in relation to any children that Emma might have, and their children's children. In other words, Thomas wanted to ensure that, lacking a male heir, his surname and coat of arms would pass to his descendants through his daughter. Such 'name and arms' clauses were a means by which testators could attempt to ensure that the family name passed with the family money. But it was not normal practice for a testator to oblige a man of such high rank as Henry, heir apparent to the Earldom of Exeter, to adopt a different surname and coat of arms!

A decade later, the writer Fanny Burney was to depict the problems that such clauses might provoke in her 1782 novel *Cecilia*: the eponymous heroine is an heiress, but her entitlement to the £3,000 per year bequeathed to her by her uncle is conditional on any future husband taking her name. The man she loves, Mortimer Delville, sees this clause as an insuperable obstacle to their union, given the antiquity of his own name. After secret marriages, many misunderstandings, and madness, the attempt to keep the family name alive in this way is roundly condemned:

> The whole of this unfortunate business... has been the result of *pride* and *prejudice*. Your uncle... began it, by his arbitrary will, as if an ordinance of his own could arrest the course of nature![40]

The likelihood of a Cecil, and future Earl of Exeter, giving up his family name was an even more unlikely prospect than in Burney's novel. Happily for the young couple, though, there was no question of Emma's entitlement under her father's will being forfeited. Whether by accident or design, her father had not stipulated what would happen if any future husband did *not* take the name of Vernon—and in such cases the courts assumed that the testator did not intend that the estate should be forfeited if his direction over 'name and arms' was not fulfilled.

Under the terms of Henry and Emma's marriage settlement, each was to receive considerable financial advantage from the marriage. Henry was to receive a sum just short of £2,000 per year from the Hanbury estates, the most that could be granted to Emma's husband under her father's will. Emma, in turn, was to receive £1,000 'pin money' (a personal allowance) from the Exeter estates and the use of the Cecil family jewels.

So was Henry and Emma's a love match, or one dictated by financial considerations? Historians have not been kind in their verdict on any of those involved. One describes Emma's mother as 'a silly, socially ambitious woman' and suggests that she 'lent heavily upon her to marry Henry Cecil'.[41] Nonetheless, the same historian noted that one of Emma's trustees and guardians 'was opposed to [the marriage] and would have backed her up if she had offered resistance.'[42] The trustee in question was Dr Treadwell Nash, who viewed Henry as 'an irresponsible young spendthrift who in no time at all would make hay of her fortune.'[43] Yet of course the marriage might well have been motivated by both affection and prudence, as was common at the time:

> Because financial negotiations were concomitants of virtually every aristocratic marriage, they are easily mistaken for causes... the details of any marriage settlement would be dictated by "the spirit of collateral calculation", but that does not mean that the same spirit had dictated the initial choice of marriage partners.[44]

Freedom of choice was not incompatible with making a suitable choice, and, as has been pointed out, 'there is no reason to believe that most aristocratic sons and daughters did not subscribe to the prevailing ethic in favour of marriages of equal rank, nor that they did not attach similar importance to considerations of status and fortune.'[45] The Enlightenment ideal was money *combined* with affection, as articulated by Eliza Barter, the heroine of a rather bad novel entitled *The Marriage Act*:

> I will never marry for Love, to lie upon straw; or marry for Title, without that Passion to improve it.[46]

And does not everyone's favourite heroine Elizabeth Bennett begin to pay attention to the favourable reports of Mr Darcy once she has seen his house and realised what £10,000 per year means in practice?

These considerations were reflected in the proportion of aristocrats who chose a spouse from within the peerage. Within Henry's particular generation of earls (or earls-to-be) it amounted to one-third, which was on the high side considering the small and select group who would have been eligible brides. But wealth might compensate for lack of rank: a third of those peers who married commoners wedded an heiress.[47]

So let us hope that when in May of 1776 Henry and Emma married at the church of St George, Hanover Square—in the presence of her mother and his uncle Brownlow, and with youth, rank and wealth on their side—they were looking forward to a long and happy life together.

The church of St George, Hanover Square, where Henry and Emma married in May of 1776

chapter 2

The Runaway Wife

As I was undressing to go to bed, Emma came suddenly into my room, apparently frantic, and related to me in a broken and almost incoherent discourse, that she had been unfaithful to my bed.[1]

So in June of 1789 began the dramatic turn of events that was to alter Henry's life forever.

Emma's agitation was not due solely to her infidelity. It transpired that the affair had been going on for some time: for five years she had been in love with the local curate, William Sneyd. He, it would seem, had tried to resist her—or was Emma merely trying to shield him in telling Henry that 'she had used every art she was mistress of to subdue the object of her affections'?

When William had eventually given in, the psychological impact on him had been dramatic: Emma reported to Henry that

> the situation she had brought Will [Sneyd] into had such an effect on his mind, that he was near going distracted; that he had procured the means and determined to destroy himself: that she had done the like and had been determined to follow his example if she could not dissuade him from his purpose.

But she had tried to persuade her lover to run away with her rather than doing away with himself, and their elopement was planned to take place during an intended visit to the town of Dudley, some twenty miles distant. Upon this being postponed, William could bear the suspense and conflicting emotions no more: his mind gave way and he was confined to bed.

Emma's guilt and concern was all directed towards William rather than her husband. It was she, she told Henry, who had made William promise to go off with her, and 'as she had been the sole cause of his misery and loss of reason, she was determined at all costs to dedicate the rest of her life to the care of him.'

Henry's first reaction was one of disbelief. 'I did not give credit to all she said, nor could I give up my opinion of her so suddenly.' He persuaded Emma to retire to bed, but the next morning she got up and told William's sister-in-law what had happened 'and did more fully acknowledge her connection and resolution.' Still not convinced, Henry went to Lichfield, where William had been taken to recover with his family, 'but there I heard the fatal truth confirmed.'

So where had it all gone wrong? The early married life of Henry and Emma had been marked by tragedy. A son had been born to them at Hanbury Hall on May 20th, 1777. The bells had rung out to welcome his birth, and he had been baptised in the church there in the name of Henry Vernon Cecil—a name which gave at least some weight to the wish of his maternal grandfather that Emma's children should bear the name Vernon. But baby Henry was not destined to carry on the family name. Less than two months after his birth, he died. There were to be no more children.

Despite their wealth, Henry and Emma had also run into debt, an eventuality which one man at least had expected. Treadwell Nash—who alone among Emma's trustees had opposed the marriage—later wrote that 'Henry Cecil is an instance of the idle extravagance of the present age, this young man when he married had a clear income of £9,000 a year, viz. £6,000 from his wife's estate, and £3,000 a year allowed by Lord [Exeter] with the whole of his Lordship's estate settled on him. In the space of about 4 years, besides the income, he had run near £40,000 in debt, which having no means of satisfying except by granting annuities at 5 or 6 years' purchase, his present income is reduced to about £2,000 a year.'[2] When their matrimonial problems became public in 1791, one newspaper similarly claimed that Henry alone had 'run through the greater part of both' the estate and cash,[3] but another blamed both him and Emma.[4]

On the positive side, much had been achieved at Hanbury Hall. Rooms had been improved and enlarged, with the parlour and an adjacent withdrawing room being knocked into one and the resulting room being decorated with a neo-classical frieze and new chimneypiece.[5] Henry not only undertook exchanges of land to consolidate the estate but also sponsored the Hanbury Enclosure Act in 1781.[6] On October 28th, 1786, he was appointed as Deputy Lieutenant in the County of Worcestershire, a military commission with a primarily civic role, and a role he already performed for Lincolnshire. He may well have been as shallow and pleasure-loving as some historians have suggested, but his public role should not be overlooked.[7]

His private conduct is more difficult to evaluate. Treadwell Nash, still hostile to Henry, suggested that he had subjected Emma to 'repeated ill-usage of all kinds' and driven her to 'Norris's drops and Madeira' as a result.[8] (The former were sold as 'an almost infallible remedy' for colds and fevers 'and also Complaints in the Bowels', and were reassuringly described as being 'as innocent as milk'. In fact, the toxic metal antimony they contained could cause heavy vomiting and diarrhea, and, if taken over long periods of time, could lead to other problems.)

So what of the man who had ousted Henry in Emma's affections? William Sneyd had been born in 1757 and baptised at the church of St George, Hanover Square (where Henry and Emma would later marry). While his pedigree was not quite that of Henry or Emma, he came from a good family. The Sneyds could trace their lineage back to the thirteenth century, had owned land in Keele since the sixteenth, and there was even a distant relationship with the Vernon family on Emma's mother's side.[9]

William's father, Major Edward Sneyd, had served in the Royal Horse Guards and as a gentleman usher to the King, before marrying Susanna Cooke and setting up home in Lichfield. Ten older sisters had preceded William and his older brother Edward into the world, although four of them had died in infancy. He, however, was the last of the family, as his mother had died shortly after giving birth to him.

To lose a parent early in life was by no means unusual in eighteenth-century England, and there was plenty of support for the Sneyd children. Growing up, they formed part of an intellectual circle in Lichfield that included the natural philosopher Erasmus Darwin and the poet Anna Seward, as well as the writer Thomas Day and inventor Richard Lovell Edgeworth.[10] The Sneyd family was apparently renowned for its good looks, and William's elder sisters Honora and Elizabeth in particular certainly seem to have had their fair share of admirers. But the shadow of consumption hung over the family, with Honora dying of the disease in 1780, less than seven years after her marriage to Edgeworth.

At the time of Honora's death, William was beginning to carve out a good career for himself. Educated at St John's College, Cambridge, a few years after Henry had himself studied there, he was awarded his degree in 1778 with the rank of 'Twelfth Wrangler', that is to say, he graduated as the twelfth best student of mathematics—not stellar, but enough to secure him a college fellowship.[11] He was awarded an MA in 1781, and on June 24th of that year was ordained in Trinity College Chapel as a deacon in the diocese of Peterborough. A year later, he was fully ordained.

The year 1783 saw Sneyd being appointed to a curacy in Hanbury, where the rector, the Reverend William Burslem, himself a fellow of St John's College, had decided that he needed some assistance. William took up lodgings at a farmhouse in the parish, and on April 3rd, 1783, conducted his first marriage at the beautiful hill-top church of St Mary the Virgin.

William's relationship with the Cecils began slowly. Henry—being, in the words of the later trial, 'a man of good fortune and of a very liberal disposition'—occasionally asked Sneyd to dinner. Their friendship developed upon further acquaintance so that, when Henry was in the county, Sneyd would dine at Hanbury Hall three or four times a week, 'until at last he became in a manner to be considered as a part of the said Henry Cecil's family'. When the weather was inclement he was often accommodated with a bed rather than risking his already frail health by returning home. His brother Edward and sister-in-law Maria were also invited to stay at Hanbury Hall on a regular basis.

Clergymen of the late eighteenth century, as a result of their social position, often mixed in circles to which they would not otherwise have been invited. The novels of Jane Austen are filled with examples: the toadying Mr Collins in *Pride and Prejudice* being the prime example, pathetically grateful for the occasional invitation to dinner at Rosings Park from Lady Catherine de Bourgh, or being asked to make up her pool of quadrille when no one better is available.

Acceptance did, however, depend on one knowing one's place, as Mr Elton finds out in *Emma* when he has the temerity to propose to Emma Woodhouse. Exasperated that her attempts to make a match between him and her friend Harriet have failed, Emma fumes that he 'should suppose himself her equal in connection or mind!'[12]

In the case of William Sneyd and his real-life Emma, of course, self-interest would have had the opposite effect. Her social standing and marital status, not to mention his ordination, would all have acted as deterrents to the young curate. But it is easy to understand how misunderstandings might have occurred. Young William, after all, had grown up with numerous older sisters: miles from home, he perhaps regarded Emma, two years his senior and married to his friend and patron, in a similar light and enjoyed an easy, and in his view fraternal, relationship with her as a result. Emma, an only child, would have had little experience of a relationship of this kind, and it was consequently all too easy to interpret friendship as something more.

And of course we need to judge William's feelings and motivations by the standards of his time, not by ours. There is sometimes a perception that people in the eighteenth century were more tolerant of sexual misdemeanours than were the upright Victorians. But the affairs of certain high-profile aristocrats should not lead us to assume that they were typical. While the term 'gallantry' was regularly used at this time as a euphemism for sexual promiscuity among what has been termed 'the rich and infamous', it was a term with specific class connotations.[13] One correspondent to *The Times* wrote on March 27th, 1786, to ask whether it would ever have occurred to 'any man of middling life, and common under-standing, that the seduction of married women, and of maids, was a harmless piece of amusement, and necessary to finish the education of a Gentleman?'[14] Such seduction might have been expected of a youthful aristocrat, but it was certainly not what was expected of a man in William Sneyd's social position.

When precisely the affair began we do not know. Emma's confession to Henry that she had been in love with William for five years indicates that she must have fallen for him in 1784, the year after he had arrived in Hanbury. But the evidence also seems to suggest that for much of those five years Emma's love was unrequited. William had evidently not succumbed immediately, although the verdict of one thirteen-year-old friend of the family that he had 'never liked' Emma perhaps better reflects a teenager's inability to understand the attraction of anyone over the age of twenty.[15]

We know very little about William's feelings, although one document does cast some light on his relationship with the family. In a box of assorted writings in Worcester Record Office relating to the Hanbury estate, there is a single sheet of paper with a few lines of verse penned by William himself. The paper is unsigned, but the handwriting is distinctive and matches William's signature in the parish registers. It is not high-quality stuff—while the challenge of finding rhymes no doubt contributed to the way in which the verse lurched from idea to idea, there was no excuse for pairing 'Vernon' with 'prefer none' or 'sourly' with 'poorly'. But it gives the impression of a young man fond of society but dogged by ill-health, and struggling with some conflict between inclination, prudence and conscience.

It is of course tempting to jump to the conclusion that it must refer to his relationship with Emma. But it is not clear to whom it is addressed, or to what it refers. It begins with:

> Of all my neighbours I prefer none
> To generous hospitable Vernon
> With him I always dine at ease
> Eat what is good, drink as I please

The ambiguity lies in the fact that it refers to 'Vernon'—is this Henry Cecil (by then master of the Vernon estate) or Emma (née Vernon) or someone else entirely? And is the 'him' in the third line the same person as 'Vernon', or is William drawing a subtle distinction between the two?

Lovers have, of course, used the medium of poetry to express their feelings for the objects of their desire from time immemorial. But few, one hopes, have produced anything quite as indecisive and lukewarm as this page of doggerel. If Emma was the intended recipient, then she would hardly have been enraptured by it, since the attraction of Hanbury Hall seems very clearly to be the male company and the food and drink William enjoys there. A more prosaic interpretation is that it is simply a few lines penned to Henry to apologise for being unable to attend an evening to which he has been invited, on account of his ill-health:

Judge then how soon I'd join a party
Where all is welcome, all is hearty
If prudence check'd not inclination
While conscience spoke out on th' occasion

And yet, while 'prudence' might counsel this 'lame curate', as he describes himself, against feasting out and being 'untimely merry', and instead lead him to nurse his cough at home, the addition of the word 'conscience' does give one pause for thought. Was William conscious of Emma's attraction to him, and guilty about it? And—a final puzzle—if it was just an excuse for not attending a dinner, why did anyone think it worth preserving alongside important documents relating to the estate? Someone, at some point in time, must have thought that it was worth keeping.

Even if it was just a note to Henry, with no coded messages or subtext at all, the poem tells us that William had considerable friendship and regard for Henry. It supports the idea that William would have been resistant to engaging in an affair with Emma: after all, a man whose guilt about being unable to attend a social function leads him to spend time writing even bad verse by way of apology does not seem like a man who would lightly embark on an adulterous affair with the wife of the friend in question.

So, while William's guilt, mental distraction, and threats of suicide might suggest something more than a brief relationship, it is equally plausible that his breakdown was triggered by his giving in to Emma, especially if he had previously regarded her in the light of an older sister, and by his betraying his role as a guest in Henry's house, as well as his status as a man of religion.

Differing accounts also exist of how the affair was discovered. Most, drawing on later trial documents, suggest that it was William, rather than Emma, who confessed to Henry. But this is rather difficult to reconcile with the account that Henry subsequently gave the Reverend Burslem. After all, if William had already told him of the affair, then he would hardly have been as incredulous when Emma made her confession. And given the fact that Henry subsequently travelled to Lichfield—where William had been taken to recover from his breakdown—to find out whether the story was true, also strongly suggests that the first communication had come from Emma. As we shall see, however, all of the parties had good reason to present a slightly different version to the court.

However the discovery was made, Henry did not want to give up on his marriage. As he later told Burslem, he informed Emma that he 'would do every thing in my power, that she wished, consistent with my Honor, to alleviate her sufferings'. He proposed first of all that they would continue to live under the same roof and keep up the appearance of being married—as long as she would break off the connection with William Sneyd. This being rejected by her, he suggested an alternative: that they should live separately and he would conceal the reasons for the separation, even going so far as to take the blame for it upon himself. But since a condition of this was her giving up William, Emma still refused. As Henry sadly noted in his letter to Burslem: 'Monday the 15th June was fixt on for our separation.'

In the meantime, however, the guilt-ridden William was proving resistant to the idea of joining Emma. The letters that she received from Lichfield indicated that he 'declined joining her & indeed that he was not fit to be trusted alone.' Undeterred by William's reluctance and suicidal despair, Emma still begged to see him just one more time. It was eventually arranged that William would be brought from Lichfield to a hotel in Birmingham, and that Henry and William's sister-in-law Maria would accompany Emma to see him there. As Henry noted, 'her distraction was such, I could not refuse.' He even hoped that she might alter her mind after she had seen William. 'All the way thro this dreadful affair', Henry wrote to Burslem, 'I determined as long as she stay'd with me to endeavour to conceal my misfortune and keep up appearances with her.'

On June 12th, Henry and Emma, together with Maria Sneyd, set out for Birmingham, some twenty miles from Hanbury Hall. It had been arranged that the rendezvous would take place at the Hen and Chickens, a coaching inn situated at the lower end of New Street.[16] Emma and William were allowed to see each other alone in order to say their goodbyes. Maria and her husband Edward, who had brought William from Lichfield, stayed in the adjoining room for a while but then decided to go shopping.

When they returned, Emma and William were gone. They had taken advantage of Edward and Maria's brief absence to make their escape in a horse-drawn carriage. Upon learning of this, the abandoned Henry tried to persuade himself that this had been an impulse rather than a deliberate deception:

> I cannot think she had premeditated the scheme, as she had neither provided clothes or money, and had also promised me to return.

But Emma was never to return. And Henry decided to turn his back on the home and the life that they had shared together. At some time between mid June and early July, he left Hanbury Hall—and his very identity—behind him.

chapter 3

Rural Tranquility

Nobody knew Henry's whereabouts. The newspapers reported that he had gone to the Continent.[1] Some of his biographers have him going to Burghley, but later letters indicate that he did not see his uncle at this time. But he did not simply disappear from his old life without trace. Arrangements were made with Henry's close friend, the rector of Hanbury, the Reverend William Burslem, that Burslem would pay off Henry's debts from the rents on the Hanbury estate.[2] Even Burslem, though, was not permitted to know where Henry was. And the letter that Henry wrote to him on July 23rd, 1789, was distinctly cagey as to his location: his reference to 'my friends in England' and his noting that 'I hear much of the French politics, but am out of the way of the riots' might even have been intended to convey the impression that he had indeed left the country and was close to the events of the French Revolution, which had only recently erupted with the storming of the Bastille nine days earlier. But at least he could reassure Burslem that all was well:

> An opportunity offering of having a letter conveyed to London I am only thankful to Providence that I can let you know that my mind is become tranquil and my body settled in a retired pleasant situation in the Country far from any large town, where I have taken some land and pass my time in constant employment and exercise. My family, name and situation is perfectly concealed from my neighbours, I don't even allow myself to be called a Gentleman, so determined am I to live secluded and sequestered from general society.

Eager for reassurance that his friends and family were also in good health, Henry asked his friend to place letters in a newspaper. Since, however, he could not guarantee obtaining the paper in question on a regular basis, he begged Burslem 'don't neglect to insert your letters every month until you hear or see an answer from me.' Equally eager to retain his anonymity in his rural retreat, he enclosed a letter to his uncle Brownlow in the missive to Burslem: this concealment was necessary 'that my connection with him, as a great man, may not be known to the bearer of this to London.'

So where precisely *was* Henry? Somewhere entirely unexpected, it turns out—a small village fifty miles from Hanbury Hall. While he does not mention Great Bolas in his letters to Burslem or give any indication of where in the country he might be, we know from the marriage register of the parish that he was already there at the time of his first letter to Burslem: on July 18th, 1789, he acted as a witness to the marriage of Sarah Massey and Mr Francis Light of the nearby village of High Ercall, suggesting that he had been in Great Bolas long enough to become known. He was, however, not known as Henry Cecil, signing the register instead with the less distinctive name of 'John Jones'.

Precisely how long he had been there has been a matter of some dispute among Henry's chroniclers. One has suggested, with apparent precision, that 'the mysterious stranger's first appearance at Bolas... was late in November, 1788, about eight o'clock pm, in a heavy driving snow storm.'[3] This indeed was the tradition both within the Hoggins family and in the village, according to another writer who spent much time investigating the family background.[4] But, given that we know that Henry must have arrived there in either late June or early July of 1789, snow seems unlikely. The Reverend Fletcher nonetheless did his best to hold on to the romance of the image by suggesting that Henry came to Great Bolas *before* Emma's elopement: 'presumably his wife's affections had been alienated from him and given to the Rev. William Sneyd before June, 1789... and this unpleasantness at Hanbury might have caused him to leave home as early as November, 1788, the date when the family assert that the mysterious stranger came to Bolas.'[5] This might have been plausible were it not for the very clear evidence of Henry's letters, and so family tradition must be discounted in this case.

Other writers, while more accurate on the dates, have similarly been unable to resist the temptation of adding climatic details: one has Henry arriving on horseback in the driving rain[6]—all too plausible for an English summer—while another puts his arrival a little later, and the only clouds are the clouds of dust rising in the wake of his cart.[7] A third hedged his bets by having Henry arrive on a fine evening with a thunderstorm threatening that leads him to seek shelter for the night in Great Bolas.[8]

Nor do any of the accounts agree on where Henry did seek shelter. Some have him putting up at the local inn, others have him begging accommodation from the Hoggins' family and sleeping in a chair in the parlour on that first night, having caught a tantalising glimpse of an attractive young girl helping her mother cook the family dinner. This latter version has the virtue of killing two birds with one stone, in suggesting where Henry first saw Sarah. But this too has been the subject of much dispute. Did their eyes meet across the pews in the village church?[9] Or was she, as another chronicler suggests, up to her elbows in suds, helping her mother with the washing that they took in to meet ends meet? Or do such accounts simply reflect the writers' desire to contrast Sarah's simplicity and domesticity with the worldliness of the adulterous Emma? The well-known radical writer William Cobbett, who later wrote of meeting his future wife in America in the late 1780s, drew on such ideas when he recalled in a book of advice for young men:

> When I first saw my wife, she was *thirteen years old*, and I was within about a month of twenty-one. ... In about three mornings after I had first seen her, I had, by an invitation to breakfast with me, got up two young men to join me in

my walk; and our road lay by the house of her father and mother. It was hardly light, but she was out on the snow, scrubbing out a washing-tub. 'That's the girl for me,' said I, when we had got out of her hearing.[10]

Admiring her industriousness and her beauty, Cobbett resolved that she would make an excellent wife. Similarly, in Walford's version of Henry's story, written in 1877, Henry was ensconced in the Hoggins' cottage from the moment of his arrival in Great Bolas, a distant glimpse of Sarah washing up in the kitchen having 'fairly enchained his eyes and his heart.'[11] It was an image with a long romantic pedigree, and as such it should be considered unlikely that it reflects the true nature of Henry and Sarah's first meeting.

And just to add to the uncertainty surrounding Henry's sojourn in Great Bolas, we have a whole range of suggestions as to who the villagers thought he was. One of Henry's biographers has him claiming to be an undertaker, on the basis that:

Possibly such a vocation might serve to account for the air of tender melancholy which seemed to surround him; or possibly the word might have been meant as a gentle hint to Sarah Hoggins that, stranger as he was, he was ready to undertake any office, however new to him or he to it, in which she herself bore a part.[12]

If this is the only basis for thinking that Henry made such a claim it seems a thin one. Not only would the hint about 'undertaking' have been too subtle for most to catch—it has the ring of a cryptic crossword clue rather than a chat-up line—but if one was going to invent an occupation to impress a young village girl, we might imagine that one that involved interring corpses seems an unlikely and macabre choice. However, there was at the time a vogue for melancholic subjects, like the immensely popular poem *Night Thoughts*, written by Edward Young in 1742, and Thomas Gray's *Elegy Written in a Country Churchyard* of a decade later. Taking grief as their subject and situated in poignant locations, at dusk or night time, these poems were part of the 'graveyard school' that remained popular throughout the century. It is therefore not too far-fetched to think that Sarah might have been attracted by the romantic melancholy of Henry, who surely did carry with him a cloud of sadness after seeing his marriage collapse so dramatically.

Other biographers have Henry passing as a landscape painter—a more romantic pursuit, certainly, but one for which there is equally little evidence. Still more romantic is the idea that the villagers thought Henry was a highwayman. This, in Walford's account, is how they rationalised his sporadic absences from the village and the fact that he tended to return with considerable sums of money:

> They put the money and the absences together, and they whispered the result to one another. They felt sure Jones was a highwayman, and possibly the tortuous and tree-darkened lanes, and the stories of highwaymen and footpads on the roads around Bolas Magna may have made the robber idea unpleasantly credible.[13]

Yet Walford immediately undermines the likelihood of the villagers holding such a belief when he adds that they 'probably… did not reflect that such a sparse country, so rarely visited by strangers, would not support a single footpad unless he possessed a large capital and could afford to abide the event.'[14] After all, the one indispensable requisite to be a highwayman is a highway! Romantic though it might be, the idea that the villagers thought Henry a highwayman is nothing but a flight of fancy. In short, there is no real way of knowing when precisely Henry arrived in Great Bolas, how he spent his first few weeks there, or whether the villagers thought he was an undertaker, an artist, or even a common criminal. But we do have an insight into Henry's feelings at this time—or rather as much of those feelings that he chose to relate to the Reverend Burslem.

If the villagers were suspicious of him as an incomer without any obvious source of income, this does not seem to have struck Henry. Come September, he was writing in glowing terms of the way in which he had been received in the village:

> The manner in which I am received and treated by those around me is truly pleasing to me. I am so proud of it I can not help boasting of it; for as no worldly pomp surrounds me; no title, no family, no connections and no riches appear belonging to me, my behaviour alone must principally cause the attentions that I receive.[15]

For a wealthy young man, brought up to privilege from birth, the shock of being jilted in favour of a poor curate must have been devastating, and it was some comfort to him that the villagers in his new abode seemed to like him for who he was. The depth of the hurt he had felt is hinted at in the reasons he gave to Burslem for not disclosing his address and communicating only through the newspapers:

> I dare not yet permit you to write to me, as my mind is not strong enough to hear unwelcome news, and nothing very material can pass thro' the medium of a newspaper to hurt me: if, however, I find it does, I can defend myself against that, by never looking at them—plain matter of fact business, I can always attend to if necessary; but I shall feel hurt if I am applied to on any business that can be done without me, for I look upon myself as gone from the world never to return.

His focus was on recovering from the drama of Emma's elopement:

> I enjoy a tranquil happiness I little expected... I fill up my time in a rationable manner, and neither despond or am low spirited. Nothing now could add to my happiness but the society of relations and friends I love, for I wish for nothing else, but as man cannot enjoy all he wishes for,

> I must have patience and be thankful to Providence for the many comforts I am permitted to have.

The passing reference to 'tranquil happiness' may give us another clue as to why Henry had decided to put down shallow roots in Great Bolas, to spend his time among simple rustic folk, and be so captivated by the Hoggins' cottage and its fair inhabitant. Retiring to a cottage in the country was a very fashionable pastime for Georgian gentlefolk. The story *Benevolence Rewarded; or, The History of Miss Harriot Worthy. A Moral Tale*, published in the *Lady's Magazine* in 1780, described the twenty-six-year-old Mrs Worthy, whose husband Henry had died, leaving her with little money. She thus determined on retirement 'that she might find greater leisure for the practice of maternal duties'. She left her elegant abode in the metropolis and went to a neat little cottage in Devon, taking her favourite domestic to attend to her little daughter Harriot.[16] As historians have observed, it was no mere fancy that the author chose a cottage as Mrs Worthy's retreat, for the cottage was a 'symbol of retirement and romantic love which flourished in the tourist's view as an idealised destination'.[17] The 1780s was the peak of the culture of 'sensibility', a style of thinking and behaving which had enraptured a generation of educated, elite people from the professional and landed classes.

The Enlightenment which flourished across Europe from the mid eighteenth century brought with it this fashion for sensibility and a love for Nature that conquered all before it. Following the advice of the philosopher Jean-Jacques Rousseau, the refined and sensitive sought out the wonders of Nature in its purity and goodness as the opposite to the World with its corruption and debauchery. Painting and drawing rural scenes and pretty cottages with roses round the door was one way to live the dream; so too was writing poetry, and following in the melancholic footsteps of Thomas Gray's *Elegy* by tramping through picturesque, rustic churchyards.

'Sensibility' was all about feeling. The Scottish writer Henry Mackenzie had published the sentimental novel *The Man of Feeling* in 1771, and popular periodicals like *The Lady's Magazine* published hundreds of serialised tales of swooning genteel young men and women, shedding tears over each other and over poor folk. Readers were moved by family scenes of wholesome goodness, and these families were often depicted in the countryside. For the mostly urban elite who spent time doing business in the city, shopping, and following 'the Season', simple country people came to embody all that was natural. Genteel folk bought prints of these rural scenes and cottages, and cried when the idealised labouring ranks were depicted as in need of charity. Dairymaids were imagined as ideals of beauty and populated Georgian art: Gainsborough's 1755 work *Landscape with a Woodcutter Courting a Milkmaid*, for example, portrays a beautiful milkmaid being admired by a young man. Aristocratic women adopted pastoral dress, and Mary-Antoinette went one better in France when she had a dairy built in which to enjoy an idealised and sanitised version of rural pastimes.

Alongside the sentimental imagery of bucolic life there also existed a rather eroticised version for male connoisseurs, who saw in the young milkmaid and the farmer's daughter objects of desire and sexual attractiveness: one of the stereotypes of the age was the simple country girl who came to London only to be corrupted into prostitution. William Hogarth's *A Harlot's Progress* famously depicted this sad decline, while John Cleland's erotic novel's eponymous heroine Fanny Hill was a voluptuous country maid who enjoyed numerous sexual exploits in the capital.

So Henry, in rejecting the life of the aristocrat in favour of rural bliss, was in fact following a well-trodden and almost clichéd path. Did he intend this to be a permanent change? His next move certainly suggested that he intended his stay in Great Bolas to be of some duration, as he purchased a plot of land and began to build a new house upon it. As early as

September of 1789 he was telling Burslem that he had 'taken land enough to support me in the manner I wish to live'—as well as asking for some money on which to draw, presumably to ensure that he could live in the manner he wished. By mid-November he was writing that 'une maisonette à l'anglaise—viz Cottage, has been built for me after my own plan upon a dry airy and healthy spot'.[18] No doubt Henry had a very strong idea of an idealised cottage in which he longed to escape from his other tiresome cares and responsibilities. While ruined cottages would come to be a particular source of aesthetic pleasure when in the nineteenth century the Romantics moulded the nation's ideas of beauty, in the 1780s the ideal imagined cottage was snug, neat and trim; something that would not look out of place in the pages of *Country Living* today. Its cleanness indicated its inhabitants' moral virtues.

Yet while the correspondence tells us a considerable amount about Henry's money problems, digestion, and exercise routine, it is frustratingly silent on his romantic inclinations. There is some evidence that Sarah Hoggins was not the only woman that Henry had his eye on. One Miss Elizabeth Taylor 'was heard by her descendants to say that she had always regretted the wonderful chance she had missed as a girl when she yielded to her parents' entreaties not to marry John Jones'.[19] Whether she had truly been in love with him is a matter of speculation: it would be natural for a woman, however happily ensconced at the charmingly named Buttery Farm, to have a smidgeon of regret that she was not presiding over Burghley House as Countess of Exeter. Whether he was ever in love with her is equally impossible to ascertain: one biographer paints an attractive picture of a girl 'just twenty... in the flower of her youth and good looks',[20] while another depicts a woman who 'felt in danger of being left in the lurch as a spinster'[21] and whose unattractive 'stilted elocution... self-conscious giggle... and well-worn repertoire of literary clichés' soon alienated Henry.[22]

Whatever the truth of the matter—whether Henry proposed to Elizabeth and was refused, or was merely gently discouraged from visiting the house—it was perhaps Henry's sense that more well-to-do families would not countenance a relationship between their daughters and a man with a mysterious past and uncertain prospects that led him to look further down the social scale for a new bride. Popular songs delighted in just this scenario: the song *Love in a Barn, or the Country Courtship*, for example, had a London Lord who fell for the delights of a milkmaid. Despite her duping him for £500 and humiliating him in front of the town, he is so besotted that—in the song's forty-sixth and final verse—he marries her nonetheless.[23]

But was Sarah Hoggins really a poor village girl? The precise social status of Sarah's family has also been disputed. Aggrieved by constant references to Sarah having been brought up in a cottage, one Maria Hoggins, describing herself as Sarah's only surviving niece, wrote in a local journal a century later that Sarah's parents in fact lived in the Old Manor House Farm, rather than a cottage,[24] supporting this claim on the basis that a 'mere cottage' could not have housed six sons and daughters and by telling readers how 'when a girl I loved to listen to the details and description of the old Manor House at Bolas.'[25] Of course, Maria, writing at the end of the nineteenth century, would have had no opportunity to see the Hoggins' actual dwelling, which was pulled down in 1845. And many cottages certainly did accommodate six or more children, however unlikely this might seem to those used to the luxury of space. But her claims spurred one writer whose work she had criticized to investigate further. W.O. Woodall 'spared no pains to ascertain what really was the size of this building, whether cottage or house, in which Sarah Hoggins was born.'[26] Examining the rate books for Great Bolas, he found that Thomas Hoggins was one of the smallest ratepayers in the village, paying around seven or eight shillings per year in the 1790s. And an old man who had lived in the house as a child gave a detailed description of it. It was:

> a half-timbered house [that] contained one sitting-room, one smaller, and a kitchen, and a back kitchen, and there was a pantry and two cellars downstairs…. Three steps into the yard at the back, and there was a pump, and then there was a farm-yard. Above, one room over the kitchen, one over the little room, and another over the back kitchen.[27]

While unsuccessful in gaining any accurate estimate of the size of the rooms in question, Woodall defended his use of the term 'cottage', saying rather tartly that 'I really do not know that I have committed myself anywhere as to magnitude.'

So—without descending into feet and inches—it is clear that Sarah's family home was a relatively modest one. The same is true of her family: her father, Thomas, was a small farmer and a farrier. And just how far Henry was stepping outside the norms of the time by courting Sarah can be illustrated by a detailed investigation of the marriage patterns and partners of the British peerage. Of the three hundred-plus young men born into the peerage around the same time as Henry—between 1740 and 1759—only four married a bride whose father was of the 'lowest social class'. And even this does not necessarily mean what we might take it to mean, since within the 'lowest social class' are included marriages to 'the daughters of a butcher, boatman, barber and printer.'[28] Marriage between an aristocrat and the daughter of a small farmer was so rare as to be unheard of.

Tracing Henry's intentions and actions through his letters to Burslem is no easy task, since he was understandably wary of mentioning any new relationship. By November of 1789 he was writing in praise of his neighbours as 'all very civil, well meaning, good people', and telling Burslem that 'I have quite got over the disagreeable sensation of being alone amongst perfect strangers and I am now so blended in the societies here, that I begin to feel interested in the occurrences that happen.'

At this stage it would appear that he contemplated remaining in Great Bolas—or at least anonymous seclusion—for the rest of his life, since he also alerted Burslem to the fact that he had 'made up a bundle of papers which is directed to you and will be sent to you at my decease', adding gloomily 'when you receive it, consider it a token of my death and make no further enquiries about me.'

In his next letter he was at least envisaging that he might outlive his elderly uncle Brownlow—'in case providence should so order it that I should survive my uncle, and be his heir'—but not envisaging that this would make any difference to his way of life, expressing his wish that Burslem would take on the task of going to Burghley and directing whatever Brownlow has wished to be done 'as for me.' He gave Burslem details of where he might find relevant papers and the family jewels, as well as directing which servants should be kept. Henry directed that, if Brownlow should die, any money from the estates at Burghley should be used to clear off his debts 'save £500 a year for myself and £1,000 a year for the expenses you will be at in executing my wishes; for you should reside much at Burghley and perhaps must take frequent journeys.'

January of 1790 saw a slight change in emphasis: telling Burslem of the improvement in his health, Henry noted that his mind was 'just strong enough to support me as I now am' but 'too weak to venture again, *or for some time*, into the busy world.' So he was at least beginning to leave open the possibility that he might return to the world at some point, even if not in the immediate future. A hasty note in February asked Burslem for urgent funds, some of his money having been stolen, and indicated that Henry was beginning to feel torn between the quietness of his new life and the friends he had left behind:

> If it was not for a few friends in England whom I much wish to see again, I should never desire to depart from the quiet abode I now am in, so serenely pleasant is it to

my mind. I am satisfied, for my wants are so little, that, I trust, they will easily be supplied, unless some unforeseen accidents happen; and even then I have a true friend in you to whom I can open all my mind and fly for assistance, with a certainty of your relieving me if in your power. What a comfort is friendship to the heart of us poor mortals. It is every thing to me in my present situation and must be happiness to me in all.

But life in his rural retreat was about to get a little more complicated.

Great Bolas church, where 'John Jones' and Sarah Hoggins
married in April of 1790

chapter 4

The Bigamous Marriage

I protest before God and man, that I have not an action or thought that I am afraid of concealing, that I harbour no ill will to any person... I know of nothing that I have done that should occasion my Uncle's resentment; but he may have reason to be disappointed about me. As he chooses to turn his back on me it will be nothing but self defence, if I act *only* for my *own* interest, consistent with rectitude.

So wrote Henry to Burslem, sometime in April of 1790. He was not, however, being entirely honest with his friend when he assured him that there was no reason for his uncle to resent him. For mid-way through that same month he went through a ceremony of marriage with Sarah Hoggins at the parish church in Great Bolas. Since he had taken no steps to end his marriage to Emma, this second marriage was null and void in the eyes of the law. Any children born to them would be illegitimate. Sarah would be regarded as no more than a concubine or mistress. And Henry himself had committed the crime of bigamy.

Why did he do it? Some of Henry's biographers have thought it was out of simple love for Sarah; others have suggested it was due to a much more practical consideration. One of the more romantic—and admittedly semi-fiction-alized—accounts has a long, slow romance, culminating in Henry disclosing his true identity to Sarah. She—sweet country lass that she is—is loving, supportive and immediately practical, and is willing to do 'a bit of wrong' for his sake. Henry formally asks her father for permission to marry her, and the wedding is duly celebrated with great rejoicing by all (except for her mother!).[1] Another version has Thomas setting a test for his daughter's suitor, saying that 'the stranger might have Sally if he could drive a pig across Hodnet Heath.'[2]

Yet another account, written in 1964, has an equally loving Sarah but a rather more abrupt culmination to their romance. Building on 'what was said locally a century later', this version has Henry and Sarah taking 'refuge in some secluded nook—a haystack or shed—driven there by the ferment of emotions that would no longer be denied.'[3] Into this intimate moment irrupts an irate Thomas Hoggins, armed with a gun, threatening to shoot Henry on the spot unless he promises to marry his daughter. But the idea of a shot-gun wedding should make us suspicious—this was not a theme native to eighteenth-century England, but became prominent in the twentieth century as an import from America: in the very first reference to the phrase in *The Times* in 1945, the speaker provoked laughter by contrasting the merger of companies under discussion with a shot-gun wedding 'as in the Western States.'[4]

In any case, one should always be wary of giving credence to stories circulated so many years after the events in question are supposed to have taken place. The credibility of the shotgun-wedding story rests upon assumptions about the risks that Henry was running:

> Bigamy in 1790 was considered so serious an offence that those found guilty of it were condemned to death… this gruesome possibility… gives support to the story that he was pushed into marrying Sally Hoggins at the point of her father's gun.[5]

In other words, the penalty for bigamy is said to have been so harsh that Henry must have been forced into it rather than going to the altar willingly. But what was the real likelihood of Henry actually being detected and prosecuted, and even hanged? Might he have thought that the circumstances of his particular case—his being abandoned by his wife, or even the fact that he was not using his real name—meant that he wasn't technically guilty of bigamy? And what punishment *was* he risking if he was detected and found guilty? Investigating the contemporary laws on marriage and bigamy is the best way of gaining an insight into what Henry's thoughts and motivations might have been—since, given his eagerness to conceal his bigamous marriage from former friends and acquaintances, he made no record of them at the time.

For a start, the chances of Henry's true identity and marital status being found out before the wedding to Sarah were minimised by his decision to marry by licence rather than by banns. The calling of banns was a very public event: during the Sunday morning service, the incumbent of the parish would read out the names of those to be joined in holy matrimony and ask of the congregation whether they knew of any just cause or impediment. This process would then be repeated on two further Sundays before the marriage could go ahead. Of course, it was highly unlikely that anyone who knew John Jones's true identity would happen to be passing through Great Bolas on a Sunday morning, but Henry might well have been reluctant to spend the three weeks worrying about the possibility of an objection being made.

Obtaining a licence would also have involved a process of deception, but at least it was quick. There was no waiting period as such, although the legislation tried to deter runaway marriages by stipulating that at least one of the parties should have lived in the parish where the marriage was to take place for four weeks. Once obtained, a licence allowed the marriage to take place immediately. (One late-eighteenth-century diarist recorded how, as a churchwarden, he had apprehended the young man who had got a girl in the village pregnant, accompanied him to obtain the licence, attended the wedding, and delivered the couple to their new parish—all within the same day!)[6] In Henry's case the process was not quite so speedy, but still quicker than by banns. It was on Easter Day, which fell on April 4th, 1790, that he and his future father-in-law set out to obtain the marriage licence. Unlike the calling of banns, a licence needed the authority of someone higher in the church hierarchy than the local vicar. Henry and Thomas accordingly travelled to the town of Wellington, some seven or eight miles distant—since the incumbent there, the Reverend John Rocke, had been granted the right to grant licences on behalf of the Vicar-General of the Diocese of Lichfield and Coventry. And it was before the Reverend Rocke that Henry—in the character of John Jones, yeoman—swore that there was no impediment to his marriage with Miss Sarah Hoggins, farmer's daughter, going ahead.

The process of obtaining a marriage licence was designed to impress on would-be husbands the importance of telling the truth. Not only did Henry have to swear that the details in his affidavit were true, but he also had to enter into a bond for £500. This meant, in essence, that he bound himself to pay that sum if any of the details in the affidavit turned out to be untrue, a common way of giving weight to promises at the time. Since the authorities might not be convinced that John Jones would have the wherewithal to pay this sum, Thomas Hoggins acted as his surety—although it seems highly unlikely that he would have been able to afford such a sum either.[7]

Henry could at least console himself with the fact that the legal technicalities in the licence were mostly true, even if he was not free to marry Sarah. The licence was granted on the condition that there was not any impediment 'by reason of a precontract entered into before 25 March 1754'—something that Henry could swear with a clear conscience, since he had been a babe in arms at the time. It was also granted on the condition that there was no litigation pending in any court as to any impediments—again true, since no formal steps had been taken to dissolve the marriage with Emma. He could even justify to himself the condition that 'neither of them be of any other Parish or of better Estate or Degree than to the Judge at granting of the License is suggested': having resided for more than the statutory four weeks in Great Bolas, he was entitled to regard himself as a member of that parish for the purposes of marriage, and even as Henry Cecil, heir apparent to an earldom, he bore no title other than the gentlemanly 'Esquire'. As for whether there were 'any other Lawful Causes Whatsoever' why Henry should not marry Sarah—well, it would not convince a court, but he was the one who had been deserted by his wife, wasn't he?

And so, nine days after the licence had been granted, on Tuesday, April 13th, the wedding took place at the parish church of St John the Baptist. The timing of the ceremony is a further indication that Henry was keen to marry without too much publicity. At the time, Sundays, rather than Saturdays, were the most popular day of the week for weddings, this being the one day of leisure that everyone had, as well as being indicated by the rubric of the Church of England as the appropriate day to wed. But at the same time, weekday weddings were not so unusual—particularly for those marrying by licence—as to attract any undue attention and comment. The witnesses to the wedding were John Picken, Sarah's uncle-by-marriage, and Sarah Adams, who is thought to have been a schoolfellow of Sarah.[8] The fact that her own father was not one of the witnesses can be explained by the fact that he appeared to have hurt his hand, his attempt at a signature to the affidavit accompanying the marriage licence having been at odds with his usual competent handwriting.

Given the speed and relative privacy of the marriage it was unlikely that its bigamous nature would have been discovered in advance of it taking place. But what was the risk of it being discovered *after* it had taken place? By the time of his wedding, Henry had been residing in Great Bolas for three-quarters of a year, undetected and unsuspected to be any more than John Jones. He had bought land and a house in Great Bolas. Did he intend, at this point, to stay there and never resume his true identity?

His letters to Burslem suggest that he did not. His occasional panegyrics on the simple country life were mixed in with clear indications that he still hoped to become Earl of Exeter. Only a few days before he had obtained the licence to marry Sarah, at the end of March, 1790, he had written to Burslem to authorise him to employ 'some professional Man to initiate the proper steps for the obtaining a divorce betwixt myself and my now wife Emma Cecil.'[9] By April, however, he was vacillating about this, on account of what it might mean for his inheritance. Complaining that his uncle Brownlow had turned his back on him, he demanded of Burslem:

> Does it not seem that his anxiety to find me out was only that you might get a proper authority to carry on a divorce? As soon as you had that, he had no more to do with me. Now if in fact by a divorce he should have sole powers to leave the Burghley estate from me, ought not I to prevent that if possible? and stop the divorce![10]

But even if Henry was worried about being disinherited, it might well have seemed to him that it was already too late to change his mind. Even if the ceremony had not actually taken place by this point, reneging on his promise to marry Sarah could have exposed him to an embarrassing action for breach of promise of marriage. And if the bigamous ceremony had already taken place, honour dictated that he take steps to free himself from his first marriage as soon as possible and remedy the situation. Begging Burslem to tell him what to do, he asked for any future letters to be directed to him at a new location:

> I must alter the mode of your address to me as I cannot stay here any longer. Direct your next to Mrs Eliz: Wayley, London to remain at post office till called for.[11]

Whether written before or after his marriage to Sarah, this was not the letter of a man planning to remain in rural retirement. The fact that he was intending to go to London—where he would, of course, need to resume his identity as Henry Cecil—raised the risk that his double life would be revealed.

So why, if Henry had already decided to take steps to obtain a divorce, did he not simply wait until this was obtained and he was free to marry Sarah legally? The process of obtaining a divorce was of course cumbersome—as we shall see, proceedings in the church courts for separation had to be accompanied by a civil suit for 'criminal conversation', before Parliament could be petitioned to pass a private Act of Parliament dissolving the marriage.

There was, however, one step that Henry could have taken to reduce the risk he was running. Even though he would only have been free to remarry validly once the private Act of Parliament had been passed, he could have married Sarah at an earlier stage without technically being guilty of bigamy in the eyes of the law. For, under the statute of 1604 that governed this crime, a person who remarried after obtaining a separation order from the church courts would not be guilty of bigamy. The marriage to Sarah would, however, still have been void. Merely living apart from one's spouse without a formal sentence from the church court, as Henry was from Emma, was not a sufficient defence to bigamy.

The only other legal defence was if one's spouse had been absent for seven years—but Emma had run away less than a year earlier. In one contemporary case at the Old Bailey the court gave short shrift to a man who had attempted to defend the charge of bigamy on the basis that 'his former wife had quitted him, and that he considered himself at liberty to marry again.'[12] He was imprisoned for twelve months.

It is just possible that Henry thought that the circumstances of his marriage to Sarah meant that he was not technically guilty of bigamy, despite the absence of a legal defence under the relevant statute. One case that had been attracting a significant amount of attention in the papers earlier that year had been that of one Thomas Hornby Morland, who had been unexpectedly acquitted of bigamy at the Old Bailey despite the clear evidence that he had gone through at least two ceremonies of marriage. The famous barrister Mr Garrow, defending him with his usual vigour, had tried to challenge the validity of *both* of Morland's marriages, since in each case the wife had been underage and—the marriages being by licence—had both needed parental consent. The evidence was that consent had been forthcoming for the first marriage, but the father of the second wife—who had been just a fortnight short of her twenty-first birthday—gave evidence that he would not have consented to the match. Mr Garrow triumphantly declared that his case was now made out, and the judge, with evident reluctance, ordered the jury to acquit Morland on the ground that his second marriage had not been valid.[13]

The decision understandably caused consternation among the legal profession. The prosecuting barrister had, in vain, pointed out that it would be permitting a man to escape punishment for the crime of bigamy on the basis that he had previously committed the crime of fraud, since in order to obtain a licence he must have sworn either that his bride was of age or that parental consent had been given.[14] It was also pointed out that it was self-contradictory to make the validity of the second marriage a condition of a conviction for bigamy, since by definition the second marriage was invalid on account of the prior marriage! And, as one person wrote to the editor of the *Morning Chronicle*:

> To say… that the second marriage must be formal to constitute the felony is, in my mind, to set up a ground for the uniform evasion of the law—in a case, which more than any other of the small felonies, merits the highest punishment.[15]

Another declared, still more passionately, that the decision 'places a trap to ensnare innocence and beauty in the hands of the villain and hypocrite.'[16]

Of course, Henry's situation was rather different. While Sarah was clearly underage, her father *had* consented to the marriage. The validity of the marriage would not, therefore, have been challengeable on that ground. But Morland's case raised the broader point that a conviction for bigamy might possibly be avoided if the second marriage was invalid because of a failure to comply with the formalities laid down by law. So did Henry think that by marrying in a false name his marriage to Sarah was not valid and that he was therefore innocent of bigamy?

If so, he was labouring under a mistake. Perhaps unexpectedly, the name in which he married would have been regarded as his 'true' name for the purposes of entering into a marriage.[17] English law has always taken a very pragmatic approach to names: one's legal name is the name by which one is known, regardless of birth certificate or deed poll. It was particularly pragmatic in the important matter of marriage, and for good reason: after all, if a man or woman could annul their marriage on the basis that the name by which they were known in the community was not their 'true' name, then it would be all too easy for opportunists to dupe the innocent into an invalid marriage. Since Henry had been passing by the name 'John Jones' for the previous nine months or more, this was a perfectly proper name for him to use on this occasion. In any case, the name used was less fundamental when the marriage was by licence than where its validity depended on the banns having been called. So had there not been the small matter of his first marriage, the marriage between 'John Jones' and Sarah Hoggins would have been perfectly valid.

And it would, after all, have been odd if marrying in a false name meant that men and women could escape conviction for bigamy. Reports of contemporary cases suggest that not a few assumed a false name and a new identity precisely for the purpose of committing bigamy. *The Observer* reported one case of 'a tall well-looking man, of respectable and ready address' who, it appeared, had 'made it a practice for some years past of assuming different characters, for the purpose of entrapping young girls and widows who have been left with small property.'[18] Only a few weeks after Henry and Sarah's wedding, the Old Bailey was hearing the case of James Saunders 'alias Jackson',[19] and earlier in the century Peter Delafountain—or De La Fountain, or John La Fontaine, or Peter de St Remye—had made several appearances there.[20]

That it was the identity of the person, rather than the name in which they married, that mattered for the purposes of bigamy was underlined by a case heard at the Old Bailey in May of 1790, just a few weeks after Henry and Sarah's wedding. Joseph Webb had been accused of bigamously marrying the gloriously named Benediction Buck under the name of 'William Webb', the marriage register for the second ceremony having recorded the latter name. James Atwood, the clergyman who had conducted the ceremony, was called to give evidence and admitted that an error must have been made in registering the marriage, confessing that he must have trusted to his memory at the time the entry was filled out and attempting to excuse himself on the basis of the conversation that had been going on as to whether the *bride's* name was correct in the licence. Since the clergyman was adamant that he remembered the man's face, Webb was duly convicted.[21]

Webb's case also underlines the fact that there were a variety of ways in which the fact of the crime of bigamy could be proved. Emma's absence was irrelevant for these purposes: as his legal wife she would have been debarred from giving evidence against Henry in any case. The certificate of their marriage would have been adequate proof of it. Sarah, by contrast, would have been able to give evidence of the second 'marriage'—such a marriage being void, Sarah would not have been debarred from giving evidence against Henry, since she was not legally his wife. And even if Sarah proved loyal and refused to give evidence against Henry, the second marriage could still be proved by those present, or by a certified copy of the parish register.[22]

In short, Henry was playing a dangerous game. He would have had no defence to bigamy, and was planning to return to London within a few weeks of his second marriage. And a further note to Burslem suggests that rumours were afoot as to what Henry had been doing in his prolonged absence from society. He clearly felt it incumbent upon himself to offer some reassurance.

> My dear Burs:, I can with the greatest truth say that I have in no way embarrassed my succession to the Burghley Estates, nor ever had it in contemplation. This I assert upon my honor.

But what exactly was the risk that Henry was running—what punishment might be meted out to him if he were detected and convicted of bigamy?

Bigamy was a serious criminal offence at this time, one that was potentially punishable by death. But it had been almost a hundred years since anyone had been sentenced to death for bigamy at the Old Bailey. The last reported case had been that of Mary Stokes, alias Edwards (and quite a few aliases besides, if the list of husbands was to be believed). The number of husbands was aggravated by the shortness of the marriages, with evidence being given that she had stayed with the first only eight days and another 'but one night, and run away in the morning'. She had also been convicted of bigamy only six months previously. Her claim that she thought this meant that she was entitled to marry again was dismissed, the court taking the view that 'she was an idle kind of a Slut, for she would get what money she could of them, and then run away from them.'[23] She was convicted and hanged.

From the start of the eighteenth century, however, the most common punishment meted out for bigamy at the Old Bailey was that of branding. This was partly due to broader changes in the criminal law. Legislation passed in 1706 had made 'benefit of clergy' (essentially, this meant that one could escape the death penalty if able to read a specific chapter of the Bible) available to first-time offenders for all but the most serious of crimes.

From a practical point of view, being branded with a red-hot iron upon the thumb did at least have the advantage of warning any potential future spouses that this individual might have a shady past. By the 1750s, however, such disfigurement was beginning to fall out of favour. While in the 1740s all of the bigamists convicted at the Old Bailey had been branded, in the 1750s this fell to three-quarters, and in the 1770s to less than half of this. By the 1790s none of those convicted of bigamy at the Old Bailey suffered branding, although in the provinces occasional cases might still be found, including, in 1791, that of Thomas Hornby Morland. Having been acquitted of bigamy at the Old Bailey on account of the formal invalidity of his second marriage, it was ascertained that there had been an intervening marriage to yet another woman, and Thomas was sent to Bury Assizes to stand trial there. Upon being convicted, he 'was sentenced to be burnt in the hand, which was done before he left Court, and to be imprisoned twelve months in the Ipswich jail.' The newspaper went on to report, with some satisfaction, that 'his head is to be shaved, he is to wear the habit of the prison, which is a very disagreeable one, consisting of wooden clogs, &c, and is to be allowed only two hours each day from close confinement'.[24]

The decline in the use of branding was in line with changing ideas about appropriate punishment. It may have been speeded up by the somewhat farcical outcome of the trial of the Duchess of Kingston, whose story was told in Chapter One and who, despite being convicted of bigamy by the whole conclave of Parliament, escaped this punishment by pleading her status as a peeress. In a legal system that proclaimed all were equal before the law, this was something of an embarrassment. In any case, subsequent legislation had given the courts discretion to order a wider range of punishments. The

Morning Chronicle & Daily Advertiser, commenting on the case of one John Kippax in 1779, noted that:

> The common opinion is that bigamy is a capital crime; but it appeared by the sentence passed on Kippax, to be of a much milder nature. According to a statute passed in the reign of James the first, the punishment was burning in the hand, and twelvemonths imprisonment, but a late act of parliament left it to the discretion of the court to change the branding into a fine; the deputy recorder therefore through humanity sentenced the prisoner to one year's imprisonment, and fined him one shilling.

As a result, despite the occasional use of branding, the most common punishment had become that of a fine. By the time of Henry's second marriage, around 42 per cent of those convicted of bigamy at the Old Bailey were fined. The fine might, however, be combined with a period of imprisonment: the one-shilling fine imposed on four bigamists in July of 1790 was accompanied by the harsher sentence of a year in Newgate.[25] So while the sanctions for bigamy were certainly not negligible, the risk of any form of bodily punishment was considerably reduced from what it had been in previous centuries.

But for Henry—the former master of Hanbury Hall, an MP, and the heir to an earldom—public opinion, particularly that of his peers, would have mattered just as much, if not more, than any formal legal verdict. Just how was bigamy regarded at the time? And how would the circumstances of Henry's particular case have been regarded by his contemporaries?

Much depended on the details of the case. Bigamy, after all, encompassed everything from 'accidental' bigamy, where the unwitting bigamist had assumed their first spouse to be dead, through cases of desertion or ill-treatment that had led to the victim to form a new union, to the most infamous cases of deception and fraud. This variability, along with the virtual abandonment of the more serious forms of punishment, meant that in the last couple of decades of the eighteenth century bigamy tended to be treated with more humour than other offences, especially in cases of multiple bigamy. At the Norfolk Assizes, for example, the appearance of a third and then a fourth wife had prompted the judge to ask the accused when he had intended to stop: 'I was only going on till I could find a *good* one', came the reply, to the amusement of the court.[26] *The Observer* noted jocularly of one man, stated to have had three wives living at the time of his final marriage, that 'Justice will now most probably do what *Hymen* has in vain attempted—*tie him up!*'[27] And it was often suggested that there might be a more salutary punishment than that imposed by the law. Reporting on one Coventry man who had been sentenced to two years' solitary confinement, the paper noted:

> They certainly have allotted him his time for repentance; but as this is an offence of great and growing magnitude, might it not have been well to render the punishment proportionately terrible, and locked up his three wives with him?[28]

Was bigamy really an offence 'of great and growing magnitude' during the late eighteenth century? One should of course always treat newspaper reports of an increase in crime with due scepticism (then as today), but there does seem to have been some basis for this claim. There had been just 125 cases of bigamy at the Old Bailey in the entire century before 1790. In the 1790s, by contrast, there were 43, a ten-fold increase on the 1780s. So it was certainly increasing, but even if one were to add in those cases heard at provincial assizes it was hardly at the level where it would generate a moral panic.

How common though was bigamy within Henry's own particular sphere? One commentator had complained, at the time of the trial of the Duchess of Kingston, that bigamy was 'laughed at, as an Offence, by those in the Beau Monde, who make a Jest of Matrimony itself.'[29] And if the papers were to be believed, bigamy in high life was not uncommon. The *London Evening Post* ran a story of 'a Person of Fortune [who] was apprehended in the Borough for Bigamy, in marrying three… Women within these five years.'[30] Six years later it was a 'gentleman of great property in Surrey' who had been taken into custody and charged with bigamy, his second wife apparently having been a 'Lady of fortune'.[31] At least two 'young gentleman of fortune' seem to have been taken into custody in Southwark for entering into a bigamous marriage with a lady, with the *London Evening Post* reporting the story in February of 1767 and the London Chronicle asserting, two months later, that it had happened the previous Tuesday.[32] The next year it was a gentleman lodging by Westminster Bridge who was apprehended,[33] and then one 'taken by special warrant at his lodgings in Goodman's fields, for bigamy, in marrying two ladies of fortune within the space of seventeen months.'[34] The *Gazetteer & New Daily Advertiser* then upped the stakes, reporting in 1779 on 'a genteel young fellow who, for some time past has lived in a very splendid manner at the west end of the town' being taken into custody on a charge of bigamy 'having married seven wives within these three years, the last of whom brought him a fortune of £7,000.'[35]

So it would seem at face value that bigamy was quite common amongst the higher echelons of society. But the formulaic nature of these stories, shorn of the personal details that journalists usually included in genuine reports of bigamy, strongly suggests that these may have been mere journalistic 'filler'—titillating column inches for a slow news day. Had these bigamous gentlemen of fortune really existed, one would have expected some reporting of the subsequent trial—that of the Duchess of Kingston, after all, filled many pages of the papers for several weeks. And her conviction had led to her being dubbed the 'Queen of Hell' at the time by the papers, and to her subsequent emigration to the Continent—hardly consistent with the idea of widespread toleration.

In any case, men of Henry's class and wealth usually had options available to them that meant they did not need to commit bigamy. Wealth, for example, might cushion and conceal marital breakdown. Couples might live totally separate lives under the same roof where that roof was sufficiently large to accommodate both without them coming into contact on a daily basis. Rich men whose wives had committed adultery had the option of obtaining a divorce—in that they were among the few with sufficient resources to obtain the private Act of Parliament that was necessary to do so. And those who were less concerned about establishing a legitimate heir to their estate might simply take a mistress instead.

Had Henry Cecil run away to London, rather than to remotest Shropshire, and begun a relationship with a young, lower-class woman, it would hardly have been a matter for comment. While the extent of sexual freedom in this period should not be exaggerated—'those who had free sexual lives were minorities and disproportionately male'[36]—Henry belonged to that small, privileged section of society that enjoyed a far higher degree of sexual licence than the rest of the population. The Enlightenment thinkers of the day placed great emphasis on what was 'natural' being good: since sexual pleasure was natural, surely it too was good? went the argument. Late eighteenth-century satirists such as Gillray and Rowlandson delighted in depicting the adulterous and otherwise illicit relationships of the elite—but their cartoons were intended to provoke laughter rather than moral outrage or condemnation. Men in public life might be lampooned for their infidelity and their mistresses, but they were not judged as being unfit for public office on account of their extra-marital adventures. The Duke of Grafton, for example, consorted with the notorious Nancy Parsons while ruling the country as Prime Minister, as well as obtaining a divorce,[37] while Lord Thurlow, Lord Chancellor during Henry's time in Shropshire,[38] had several illegitimate children by the daughter of the man who kept Nando's coffee house at Temple Bar.[39]

Since, for a man of status, engaging in an illicit sexual relationship with a single woman of similar class and status was not usually an option, the choice lay between adulterous liaisons with married women in society, or relationships with the sort of women that a gentleman would not be expected to marry. Some were courtesans whose roll-call of sexual partners encompassed the highest in the land; others were actresses with dubious reputations and precarious careers. Many were simply drawn from a different station in life. Some of these relationships were long-term. Some even ended in marriage. But for every Cinderella story in which a wealthy aristocrat married his long-term mistress, there were many more discarded—some with adequate provision for the future, but others not.

Elizabeth Inchbald's contemporary novel *A Simple Story* succinctly illustrates how the woman's status might affect the nature of the proposals made to her: her character Lord Margrave has already proposed marriage to a particular woman, but he then hears that she has been cast off by her father and hopes to obtain her 'upon the illegal terms of a mistress'. As he puts it, 'the discarded daughter of Lord Elmwood cannot expect the same proposals which I made while she was acknowledged.'[40]

Had Henry met Sarah—or any sixteen-year-old girl fresh from the country—in London rather than in a rural parish, he might have seduced her, or set her up in lodgings and visited her. He might even have brought her to live in his own home, and perhaps introduced her to his bachelor friends.[41] This is what Cuthbert Shafto, widowed gentleman and father of eight children, did in 1770 when he met a milliner in Hexham and fell for her. With tradespeople for her parents, Cuthbert was determined not to marry Mary Swinburne, but persuaded her to live with him as if she were his wife. Cuthbert came into his inheritance in the early 1780s and set up home in a fine mansion, and Mary, now mother to several more of Cuthbert's children, surprisingly persuaded him to legalise their relationship. Unfortunately the union went badly wrong, resulting in a separation on the grounds of cruelty and adultery by the later 1790s.[42] But it was unusual for such gentlemen to marry their objects of desire.

So in marrying Sarah rather than merely taking her as a mistress, Henry was certainly unusual. As a bigamist, however, he was practically unique in pretending to be *less* wealthy than he actually was. It was almost always, for obvious reasons, the other way round. A few decades later, another Stamford man, Charles Cave, achieved local notoriety when he was tried for bigamy. Having arrived in Carlisle in February of 1824, he put up at the King's Arms and put out that he was a man of property. His method of telling people exactly how much he was worth was ingenious: claiming to be suffering from pains in his chest, he called in a local solicitor to dictate his will. Since a husband with considerable wealth and a weak heart was an enticing combination, it was not long before Charles was eloping to Gretna Green—twelve or so miles up the road, and north of the Scottish border—with the landlord's sister, who was entitled to £1,000 upon coming of age. He proved rather more reluctant to have the marriage ceremony repeated upon the English side of the border, but was eventually prevailed upon by his new wife's friends to do so. It then transpired that it was all a pretence. Far from being the owner of Thorney Abbey, he was only a cooper. And he was already married. Not only that, but he had deserted his wife a few days before her confinement. The court sentenced him to what was by then the maximum sentence of transportation to Australia for seven years.[43]

Such stories prompt a final question. Did Sarah know that the man she was marrying was Henry Cecil, MP, heir to an earldom, and already married? Or did she marry him believing him to be John Jones? Various accounts of their relationship have suggested that Henry told her everything. Given the fact that we do not have her side of the story—and only a guarded version from Henry—we can never know for sure. For a young village girl knowingly to enter into a bigamous marriage that might leave her as a single mother of illegitimate children would have been a risky step indeed. On the other hand, it would have been clear that there was something out of the ordinary about John Jones.

And this brings us back to the issue of whether Henry was planning to remain as John Jones. One intriguing detail is the deed that was drawn up in advance of the wedding, by which 'John Jones' settled his house and land in Great Bolas on Sarah. While marriage settlements were the norm among the Cecils and the Vernons, they were certainly unusual among the Hogginses. And any marriage settlement that seemed to give the wife such a large share of the husband's assets was even more unusual: a marriage settlement was usually used to protect the wife's property from being squandered by the husband, not to transfer it from husband to wife. If Henry had been planning to remain in Great Bolas, this would have been unnecessary.

Whatever he had told Sarah about his identity and his future plans, their early married life seems to have been contented, despite certain money troubles. By the end of October, after six months of marriage to Sarah, Henry was writing to Burslem in terms that suggested he might, after all, remain in rural retirement:

> I am living in peace and cheerfulness bearing no malice or ill will to mankind, and doing as much good to my neighbours as my situation admits. And thus I trust I shall live all my life, if I can avoid the connection of wrong headed mortals, or being interested in worldly concerns. Retirement and solitude is truly my pleasure, and nothing shall draw me from it, but the certainty of affording help or happiness to others. I have long been engaged in high scenes of life, I now see the reverse, and I am clear of opinion that the lower ranks of mankind are infinitely

more happy than their superiors, and that the peasant, with house, fire and work, surpasses all in happiness.

And he closed his letter with a final line emphasising once again his own conviction that he had acted rightly in leaving Hanbury Hall and marrying Sarah:

This does not bespoke a heavy conscience.[44]

chapter 5

An Action for 'Criminal Conversation'

In the meantime, steps were underway to end Henry's first marriage. On June 26th, 1790, Henry Cecil sued the Reverend William Sneyd for adultery with Emma in a lawsuit for 'criminal conversation' (commonly known as 'crim con'). It has been noted with a touch of humour that the behaviour alleged in a criminal conversation suit was neither criminal, nor, indeed, a conversation. It was, instead, a civil suit brought by an aggrieved husband against his wife's lover to recover damages for the adultery. And it was also one of the three steps legally required for men to divorce their wives at this time, although cuckolded husbands might resort to this option even if they did not intend to proceed to petitioning for divorce, with some simply separating or, in rare cases, allowing the wayward wife to return home.

The allegation in a 'crim con' suit was, first, that the wife's lover 'with force and arms made an assault upon [the wife and] seduced, debauched, deflowered, lay with and carnally knew her.' The wife might have been an avid participant in the adultery from its outset—she might even have been the one who initiated it—but the pretext of a criminal conversation trial was that the wife's lover was the aggressor, she his passive victim. Although the language these pleas used makes the attack on the wife sound horrific, the true victim in a 'crim con' plea was supposed to be the husband, the wife being primarily reduced to the channel of the attack on him. The crime against the husband was that, as a result of the adultery, he lost his wife's 'service and society, comfort, conversation, affection, aid and assistance'—almost the entire basis of his marital happiness.[1] In these suits, the husband sued his wife's lover for monetary damages for this attack on him, his wife, and his marriage. The adultery could not be undone, but with high damages, a husband's suffering could, ostensibly, be mitigated: the sentence was then the jury's judgment on what the husband's pain and suffering were worth. For the husband to succeed, his counsel needed to depict the injury to his client as extreme; meanwhile, the defendant's counsel would try to present his client as innocent altogether, or, if that weren't possible, would try to introduce mitigating factors to keep the damages low. Damages varied widely: in the decades immediately before and after Henry's divorce, for instance, the highest damages awarded were £10,000; the lowest were ten shillings—this last being the lowest ever awarded in a case that found for the plaintiff.[2]

So, winning a case for criminal conversation against a wife's lover was the first step. Any husband intending to go on to pursue a Parliamentary divorce would certainly hope for high damages in the crim con suit, as this money could provide even those with very moderate incomes with the means to pay for the necessary trial in the ecclesiastical court and then in Parliament, where the case would be re-examined in both the House of Lords and the House of Commons. He would need to be able to pay for his counsel and to bring both himself and witnesses to wherever his ecclesiastical court trial was to take place, as well as to London for the trials in Parliament. If he won his crim con case, the defendant would have to pay court costs, and if he won in the ecclesiastical court his wife might have to pay at least some of those court costs, but of course a husband could not be sure that he *would* win. And while Henry Cecil had had considerable wealth, he also liked spending his money. So if the Reverend William Sneyd had been found liable to pay Henry a large sum in damages for criminal conversation, it would have helped Henry immensely.

In determining the appropriate level of damages in any given case of criminal conversation, a whole host of factors came into play. Typically, aristocratic husbands, or those related to the aristocracy by blood or marriage, received higher damages, anywhere from £3,000 to £10,000. As a general rule, men not associated with the aristocracy would be awarded a great deal less, often well below £700. The rationale for awarding higher damages to those of higher rank was that they suffered more from the humiliation of their wife's adultery. If the husband was of high rank and the wife's lover was well below him, the humiliation was all the more potent, although set against this was the practical consideration that if the husband wanted to collect damages awarded to him, he had to hope for an amount that the adulterer could actually pay. Conversely, if the adulterer was of high rank and the man he wronged of much lower rank, damages would not be particularly high, as though to say that such a husband could not suffer as much as his betters or that a wife from that class was not worth as much. Such were the assumptions of the English class system of the day. But Henry, as the heir to an earldom who had been cuckolded by a mere curate, would seem to have had a strong case on this point, and he might have expected substantial damages as a result.

A second factor was whether, in losing his wife and seeing his marriage crumble, a man could be argued to have lost something of great value. After all, the purpose of these suits was not only to prove that the adultery had taken place but to put a price on the husband's loss. In cases in which the husband was granted high damages, the wife was typically presented as beautiful, accomplished, loving, and, until the seduction, a paragon of virtue; the marriage had to be presented as being as close to connubial bliss as possible. The wife might thus be described as was the wife of the Reverend George Markham in 1802, as 'a Lady of great beauty and accomplishments, most virtuously educated, and who, but for the crime of the Defendant that assembles you [the jury] here, would, as she has expressed it herself, have been the happiest of womankind.'[3] In the 1797 case of Samuel Boddington, Samuel's counsel, Mr Thomas Erskine, characterized the wife in similarly glowing terms. When Samuel first saw the woman he was to marry,

Grace Ashburner, he was supposedly 'enraptured with her charms, as she then possessed indiscribable [sic] beauties, both of body and mind.' In fact, 'the inexpressible sweetness and dignity of manners,' Samuel's counsel asserted, 'rendered her irresistible. No wonder, then, that Boddington was deeply struck with this paragon of women.'[4]

It also helped the plaintiff if the marriage could be presented as a love match rather than one designed to solidify the families' rank and estates. In addition to Samuel Boddington's being smitten by Grace, their courtship was portrayed as utterly romantic, almost like something out of a fairy tale. When he first met her, she was only in England to be educated, her father living then in India. Once her education was finished, she was supposed to return home. She boarded the ship to take her back, and it embarked, but Boddington, 'almost reduced to a state of despair by the thoughts of losing her,' rushed from London to Gravesend to claim her; he 'entreated, he implored' her guardian to bring her back on shore and to write to Grace's father for her permission for the two to marry.[5] The fond couple then waited the ten months it took for her father's blessing to the match to arrive. Another equally romantic case occurred in 1808, when the Reverend Charles Massey faced down paternal disapproval and the temptation of a connection with a more eligible young woman, and

> declining the hand of an amiable and accomplished lady, refusing an ample and independent establishment, with the additional enjoyment of parental bounty and approbation, and forgoing all these advantages, Mr Massy proved the sincerity and purity of his attachment, by a generous sacrifice of fortune, to affection, and married Miss Rosslewin.

In their marriage—at least before the wife's seduction by another man—the couple's happiness

...really was unmixed, and unabating, he loving with constant and manly ardour, she with chaste and equal affection.... [They] exhibited such an example of domestic contentment and satisfaction to their neighbours, their relatives, and their friends, as to convince them, that the sacrifices he made, were not too great, that her grateful and affectionate returns to a conduct so nobly liberal, and disinterestedly affectionate were not too little.[6]

Given the powerful rhetoric that was deployed in other cases of the day, the silences in Henry and Emma's criminal conversation trial are just as significant as what was actually said. Perhaps there was nothing comparable to say about the couple's courtship, and Henry's counsel, Mr Bower, said tellingly little about Emma's beauty, accomplishments, or virtue. But he nonetheless valiantly claimed that it would be hard to imagine a better marriage. Henry, he asserted, 'lived with [his wife] for many years, in the greatest domestic happiness and tranquility,' adding that 'no two persons could live in a state of greater affection or greater harmony than Mr and Mrs Cecil.'[7] He must have known that for most of that time, Emma, at least, was not experiencing domestic happiness; for the last five, after all, she had been in love with William Sneyd. But it would hardly have helped Henry had Mr Bower made the truth known.

Another factor that was taken into account in such cases, and which should have worked in Henry's favour, was his relationship with Sneyd, as well as the hospitality Henry had shown to the curate. Being so horribly betrayed by a former friend—or, worse, a relative—could bring the wronged husband extremely high damages. Samuel Boddington, for instance, was awarded £10,000 when he sued his cousin Benjamin, who was also his business partner, for adultery with his wife Grace. Samuel's counsel made sure to stress that Benjamin breached more than an allegiance based in the men's blood and business relationships by emphasizing the fact that Samuel had extended hospitality to Benjamin, who spent many days a week in the couple's home, sharing meals with them and even sleeping there. Samuel started to suspect that Benjamin was taking more advantage of this hospitality than he ought when he saw that Benjamin was paying perhaps too much attention to Grace. He had no idea that Benjamin and Grace were already having an affair, so he proposed to his wife that they leave London for Bath and Wales for a month or more to remove her from any possible temptation to commit adultery. Benjamin could remain in charge of their thriving business. Benjamin reminded Samuel that they were expecting a large shipment of cargo, however, and suggested that he might be needed back in town when it arrived; he said he would write to Samuel to let him know if this were the case. Benjamin wrote to Samuel to let him know that the cargo had indeed arrived, but when Samuel got to their place of business, he found that the whole thing was a ruse: While Samuel was on his way back to London, Benjamin was in fact either on his way to Bath or already there, waiting for Samuel to leave so that he could elope with his wife. There was no shipment; all that Samuel found was a letter from Benjamin that read,

> When we parted last Wednesday, it was for the last time. I have deceived you in this transaction, but it is not the first time that I have deceived you. When you see my father, for God's sake, break it out to him by degrees.[8]

Samuel's barrister invited the jury's indignation by pointing out that

> when the offending party is connected by the plaintiff by the nearest ties of blood—by the sacred bonds of friendship—by the contracts of mutual interest… when these circumstances are considered—I am convinced, Gentlemen, that you will feel as I do, and that by your verdict, you will stigmatize this transaction with all the infamy which it deserves.[9]

Another case involving a man not connected to the aristocracy but who nonetheless was awarded £10,000 was Captain John Parslow, whose wife, like Samuel Boddington's, was seduced by a man close to her husband, and who, like Boddington, had Mr Erskine as counsel. In this case, the guilty party was a Francis William Sykes, who served in the same regiment with Captain Parslow and was, the husband's counsel repeatedly stressed, Parslow's 'brother officer.' Sykes may not have been a blood relative, but the relationship they shared, within the institution of the military, was seen as perhaps even closer, so that betraying it was as bad as a man's seduction of his own cousin's wife. Sykes' departure from an army officer's uprightness exacerbated the crime. Mr Erskine explained that 'as brother officers, their friendship began'; although Sykes, as an officer, should have been

> a man of openness, candour, and integrity, [he] formed a complete and striking contrast of the officer, and the man of honour; for instead of that manliness of spirit, and unwillingness to trifle with the happiness of others, he had discovered himself to be of so selfish a disposition, that he was ready to sacrifice the comforts of the dearest friend, to the gratification of his own desires.[10]

Although Sykes 'lived in the character and habits of the most friendly intimacy' with Parslow, he 'made so bad, so ungenerous, and so unprincipled an use of these advantages, that instead of expressing happiness at having the pleasure of becoming the friend of the plaintiff,' he returned Parslow's friendship by seducing and eloping with Mrs Parslow. Betraying that friendship and the bonds of officerly brotherhood most certainly contributed to the high damages he had to pay Parslow. And there were other factors here too: Sykes actually said, in the presence of others, 'I should like to debauch that woman.' He also flaunted the relationship. 'Having thus succeeded in the object of his guilty, criminal, and treacherous system,' Mr Erskine asserted, Sykes decided that he 'must proceed to make it public; thus he brings the lady in triumph to London, in his open carriage, and there vaunts of his victory.'[11]

Henry Cecil and William Sneyd, of course, were not blood relatives, nor did they share the type of bond that military men were supposed to feel towards one another. They were not even social equals: Sneyd was, after all, just a curate. Henry's hospitality to the man was simply a testament to his generosity and his willingness to patronize the curate by opening his house to him. Henry overlooked the men's difference in rank, concentrating on the fact that Sneyd was 'the son of a respectable gentleman'; to Henry, this was enough for him to treat Sneyd 'with affection and politeness.' Henry

> accordingly introduced him into his family, and received frequent visits from him: the defendant often dined with the plaintiff, and being in a poor state of health, when the weather was bad, he was constantly accommodated with a bed in the plaintiff's house, and was treated in every respect as a gentleman, and as a proper guest to visit in his house.[12]

Lord Ellenborough, presiding in another case, told his jury what the jury deciding upon Henry's case might well have been told: 'if you are satisfied that an adulterous intercourse has taken place, there has been... a violation of the strongest confidence of honour and duty between man and man—as strong as can well be imagined.'[13]

Sneyd had both broken in on a supposedly happy marriage and betrayed Henry's hospitality; that should have been enough, one would think, for to award Henry high damages. But a strong defence was mounted by Sneyd's counsel, the eloquent Mr Thomas Erskine.

Whether he represented plaintiffs or defendants, Thomas Erskine had an immense reputation for virtually transfixing juries through his charisma and courtroom performances, leading them through emotion, rather than reason, not only to accept his version of cases but also to award exemplary damages in those cases in which he represented plaintiffs.[14] Two of the men he represented as plaintiffs in the years surrounding Henry's case were, despite being non-aristocrats, awarded the very considerable sum of £10,000. His strength came from his eloquent, powerful appeals to the sentiments, whether talking about the wife's regret, the husband's misery, or the children's suffering. In one case, for example, Mr Erskine deployed this style to talk about the children the couple might have had, had it not been for her lover's interference, claiming that:

> There was every reason to believe, that, but for the intrusion of the Defendant, many children would have blessed the parents and adorned the family—Children, at once the care and happy fruits of the endearments of the nuptial bed!—Children, whose innocent appearance gave vigour to declining age, and whose engaging manners sweetened the most bitter drops of the cup of affliction!—It is for them we toil and endure the hardships of the roughest life!—it is for them we labour beyond the period at which it is natural to seek repose in retired life!—it is for them the greatest female beauty fades without regret: and... smiles in viewing, as it were, her own beauty commencing a new life! With this view the orator... slopes into the vale of years—finds in his son the orator arising, while himself is sunk in powers below the level of common conversation! Were we incapable of feeling these becoming hopes of our posterity, we should be chargeable with the appetites of brutes, and not the sublime sensations of human beings; and but for this children would be deemed a curse, instead of a consolation; the most splendid and commodious palace, without these feelings, would be more horrid than a dungeon![15]

So, given this ability to wring pathos from even imaginary offspring, how did Mr Erskine seek to defend William Sneyd?

The options for William's defence were limited. The adultery itself could not be denied, given the elopement and the testimony of numerous witnesses. Instead, Mr Erskine took the unusual strategy of claiming that it was the wife, not her lover, who was the seducer. Saying that Emma 'might be considered as a matron', and worse, that 'she was possessed of no personal beauty or attractions', he suggested that Sneyd could not have found her attractive and was more the victim than the transgressor.

Admittedly, painting the wife as unattractive was not the only way of exculpating her lover. Where the woman was deemed to be beautiful, it might be argued that the fault was 'the very powerful effect of the Lady's charms, to the *blaze* of which [the lover] was constantly exposed, … that led him to the commission of an act that must for ever render him a miserable outcast of society.'[16] One cannot help but feel a little sorry for twenty-nine-year-old Emma, given that neither counsel gave any weight at all to her personal attractions. Instead, Mr Erskine asserted that Emma took advantage of her superior status: 'from the rank and dignity which she held in the country, as wife of Mr Cecil, [she] had an opportunity of drawing into her snare an unfortunate young man who possessed an handsome person, which happened to attract her attention.'[17]

This was not the only time such a defence was made, but usually the disparity in rank was greater. In the 1791 case in which John Wilmot sued his footman, Edward Washborne, for adultery with his wife, Fanny Sainthill, the defence argued that 'the defendant would as soon dare to place his body before a cannon's mouth, loaded with ball, and just going to be fired off, as he would presume in the liberty of making the first advances.'[18] Erskine was characteristically astute in using Emma's superior rank to Sneyd's as a means of mitigating damages. In another case in which a wife thus stooped to conquer—albeit one who stooped much lower—the counsel for the defence said that she...

with a coarseness and crapulence of appetite, as disgusting
to be spoken of to others, as it is degrading and disgraceful
to herself, is admitted to have prostituted herself to the
coachman of the plaintiff, or, in the language of the Attorney
General, to have surrendered to his base embraces. It is for
the loss of such a woman—it is for the damages from the
loss, and for the depravation of a wife of such a description,
that the present action is brought.[19]

Emma had not stooped to such depths, but the jury was likely
to be suspicious of a woman whose lover's rank was below
her own.

Regardless of who initiated the affair between Emma and
Sneyd, Mr Erskine also used Sneyd's regret over the affair to
lessen the damages against him. Referring to Francis Sykes,
who had cuckolded his fellow officer, he pointed out that
Sneyd 'has no resemblance to that triumphant adulterer that
was tried by a Jury some time ago in this place, and who met
with the exemplary punishment which was due to his crime'.
Instead, 'the *present* defendant felt for the honour of his friend
as well as for his own situation.'[20] He argued that Sneyd in fact
was the one who had admitted the affair, that he did so 'in
the hour of sickness, [being] desirous of making some sort of
atonement to the person whom he had injured, and to obtain
his forgiveness.'[21] Henry's letters to Burslem identify Emma
as the one who confessed to the relationship, but it certainly
served Sneyd's case to be presented as the one who took the
initiative to do so and who was sorry for his actions and
concerned about Henry's honor. By contrasting Sneyd to the
disloyal Sykes, Erskine must have made Sneyd seem innocent
indeed.

In Sneyd's case, furthermore, Mr Erskine suggested that
Henry must have known about the relationship, or at least
that he showed 'levity'—inadequate concern for his wife's
behaviour; if so, the ensuing events would have been 'owing
to his own misconduct,' which would mean that he 'has not
a right to expect large damages from a jury.'[22] Charges of

levity had, in previous cases, decreased damages to laughable amounts. One of the most famous was Theophilous Cibber's suit against William Sloper in 1737. Cibber ostensibly went to the chamber in which his wife and her lover were in bed, bringing 'the pillow on which Sloper and his wife were to sleep together.' Damages in this case were a meagre £10.[23] In Sneyd's case, much was made of the fact that he and Emma often fished alone together as well as going on frequent walks. If Henry did not actually suspect wrongdoing, Erskine suggested, he was still to be faulted for leaving his wife alone with another man, the more so because he did so for two whole years. Of course Erskine was trying to have his cake and eat it here—if Emma were as unattractive as he suggested, then Henry would be right to think there would be little danger of an affair starting between Sneyd and Emma. He could hardly have expected that Sneyd would have tried seducing Emma or even that he would have been susceptible to seduction by her.

Erskine even implied that Henry went beyond levity to connivance, knowing about the relationship and either ignoring it or helping forward it. Such an argument could also lessen the damages awarded to the plaintiff. As Lord Kenyon asserted in another case,

> where the husband is privy to the seduction of his wife, and where the injury is owing to his own misconduct, though the person who offends is not, in the eye of God delivered from his crime, yet the husband has not a right to expect large damages from a jury.[24]

The point on which Erskine focused in Sneyd's defence was that Henry had allowed the trip to Birmingham that ultimately led to Emma's elopement with Sneyd. If Henry knew that his wife had already committed adultery with Sneyd, and, worse, was nevertheless actively bringing this adulterous wife to her lover, it would certainly look like he did not care about his wife's morality and, possibly, that he was trying to entrap Sneyd.

Erskine thus tried to prove what Henry's letters to Burslem reveal to be true: that Henry knew about the adultery already at that point. But he also had to prove that Henry really was purposely bringing his wife to, at the least, a tryst with Sneyd. If, after all, Henry really did believe that his wife was taking one last farewell of her distraught lover, he could be accused of foolishness and naiveté, but not of actually helping her elope. The levity defence might still work, but saying Henry had connived at the affair would not.

To undo the damage, Mr Bower, Henry's counsel, tried to provide a more innocent version of the trip, saying that Emma wanted 'to go on a party of pleasure to Birmingham' and that she, her husband, and Sneyd's older brother Edward left Hanbury for Birmingham together for this purpose. Bower claimed that Henry 'returned to Hanbury alone, in the evening, and Mrs Cecil was to have followed him, in company, with Mr Edward Sneyd'[25] and that when Emma did not return, Henry 'began to be anxious about her, but had no idea what was going forward.' It is hard to know how the jury would have reacted had they known the truth about this trip.

For Mr Erskine's versions of events to be convincing, he needed a witness who would corroborate that Henry knew what was going on all along. He tried to get this information out of a man who was likely to know the truth, because he saw the Cecils every day—the butler, William Jauncey.[26] But Jauncey resisted saying that Henry knew what was going on. He admitted that Henry 'knew they used to walk out together in the fields,' but, he added, 'I do not believe that he knew they used to be in private together.'

Frustrated, Mr Erskine responded: 'Sir, you are the most incomprehensible fellow I heard in my life.'[27] He pushed and pushed for the answers he wanted, even overstepping the bounds of courtroom procedure in so doing. To Erskine's leading questions, Henry's counsel Mr Bower objected that the answers for which Erskine was angling, and which he wanted to use as proof, were simply not legal evidence. Lord

Kenyon admitted Bower was correct, yet he upheld Erskine's methods as long as he could. The verbatim record of what was said gives a flavour of the atmosphere in court that day:[28]

Erskine: 'Was not the adultery of this woman, Mrs Cecil, notorious in the husband's family at the time they set out for Birmingham?'

Bower: 'I submit to your Lordship this is not evidence.'

Lord Kenyon: 'I think this question may be asked; whether it was not matter of notoriety that she was false to her husband's bed?'

Erskine: 'Was it not notorious in your master's family at that time, that this adultery had been committed, and that it had been discovered to your master?'

Jauncey: 'I have heard that it was discovered to my master.'

Erskine: 'Then you have reason to believe, from the common report of the family, that the adultery of this lady was known to her husband?'

Jauncey: 'I believe it was.'

Bower: 'I submit to your Lordship, that this is nothing like evidence.'

At this point, Lord Kenyon did remind Erskine that he had to establish 'an actual discovery' of Henry's knowledge of the relationship. So Erskine returned to his cross-examination of the butler, asking him whether he had ever heard the adultery spoken of in Henry's presence. When Jauncey replied that he had not, Erskine tried to redirect blame onto him, as though to prevent the jury from recognizing that he had failed in proving his point, demanding, 'was it like the fidelity of a servant, not to communicate such an affair to his master?'[29] Erskine then tried to insist that some of the servants must have spoken of the relationship, but Jauncey refused to help him out here too, equivocating, and saying that the servants 'did not all speak of it, because they were not all in the house.'[30] And when Erskine asked him, 'Do you know where Mr Sneyd went when he left Hanbury?' his answer was simply, 'He went into his father's carriage.'[31] Jauncey obviously did not want to do anything to incriminate his employer Henry with connivance in Emma's infidelity.

Erskine also employed his flair for the dramatic, asserting that Sneyd 'fell into the snare of this woman'[32] and that 'when the defendant recollected the situation to which he was reduced'—including loss of his position—'he fell into a delirium.'[33] He reminded the jury in similarly melodramatic words that, if they awarded Henry high damages, Sneyd would 'be utterly undone and ruined; and now he is left an awful monument—deprived of his reason, lost in his health, and miserable in the extreme.' He likewise drew on the lachrymose when he described the scene in which Henry originally forgave his wife. Once the adultery has been confessed, he said, 'she fell down on her knees, and implored her husband to allow her once more to go and see this defendant, to take her final leave of him, and to give up his embraces for ever; and that she would then return to her duty.' He then shifted tone dramatically, from the sublime to the ridiculous: Emma 'set out to find this miserable creature the defendant—a person lying in his bed—The moment she found him, she put a white coat upon him, clapt a false tail to his hair, and carried him off without delay, to Thompson's Hotel at Exeter!'[34]

Even so, Erskine was actually fairly muted in tone in the Cecil trial, or at least much briefer in his sentimental appeal than was his normal practice. Compared to his emotive discussion of the Parslows' non-existent children, for instance, his arguments in defence of Sneyd seem like weak stuff. This may have been because Erskine had not been able to speak to Sneyd about the case before the trial, as Sneyd was too infirm to come to London. But Erskine nonetheless crafted his prose to the case. He guided the jury to what he hoped they would believe by using an abrupt shift away from the melodrama of the suffering curate, delirious and penitent, to the ludicrous image of Emma's clapping a false tail to his hair and absconding with him. Through humour, he highlighted his derisive attitude to this unattractive matron so driven to ensnare her victim that she will drag him out his sickbed and make off with him. He as much as tells them that seeing Sneyd as the seducer is laughable.

In all crim con cases, after the plaintiff's counsel had set out how thoroughly wronged his client was, and the defendant's counsel had countered these arguments by asserting either that the adultery hadn't taken place or that there were strong mitigating factors, the officiating judge would address the jury before they put a price tag on the wrongs suffered by the husband. The presiding judge in this case, Lord Kenyon, was exactly the judge that a wronged husband would want to see on the bench. As the judge who heard numerous criminal conversation trials throughout the 1780s and 90s, he has been said to have 'inaugurated a reign of terror in King's Bench against adulterers.'[35] Shocked by what he saw as the spread of moral decay, he argued that it was the duty of his court 'to set an example to the nation by the infliction of exemplary punishment upon the defendant.' He coined the phrase that if a man 'cannot pay by his purse, he must pay by his person'—in other words, be sent to debtors' prison—simply ignoring the fact that he was, in effect, making a criminal case out of a civil action.[36]

In the case in which Lord Kenyon seems first to have used this phrase—the Walford case of 1789—he instructed the jury that 'they were to weigh the heinousness of the guilt, and not the extent of the Defendant's property', adding, 'God forbid, that a man who has had originally no fortune, or who has dissipated it, should be allowed to commit this offence, and should be permitted with impunity to break the peace of families.'[37] Erskine, addressing the court, asserted that in such cases, 'no jury will inquire very minutely into the extent of his property; nor will you ever think it necessary to examine, whether this capital proceeded from his father, or was his own property.'[38] In that case, the defendant was indeed 'entirely dependant on his father, and had no property of his own.'[39] The sentence nonetheless was fairly high—£3,500 in damages.

The amount awarded against another adulterer, Benjamin Boddington, was likewise punitively high—so high in fact that the rest of his family was likely to suffer as well. His counsel, Mr Law, pointed out that if damages were high, 'he must either perish in a prison, or the weight must fall on the innocent and unhappy father'; if they awarded any more they would 'by that means destroy the means of supporting eight daughters.'[40] He asked the jury to assign damages no higher than £3,000, the amount of money Benjamin had received from his father and invested in the business.[41] But the Under Sheriff reminded the jury that 'fortune can never be urged as a criterion to direct a Jury, ... [or] men without fortunes might violate the laws with impunity.' He wanted damages that 'may operate as a lesson to the world.'[42] The jury heeded this argument and, as we have seen, granted Samuel Boddington damages of £10,000.

Sneyd's family situation was perhaps worse than Boddington's; at least Benjamin's father was wealthy, so after paying the £10,000 he might still have had money for his many daughters. Erskine explained of Sneyd, however, that he was one of many children and that his father had very little property and so would be unable to pay large damages. Nor would Sneyd, a curate without any property, be able to pay 'any thing like that which a man of fortune would be obliged to pay.'[43]

One would think that, given the fact that Lord Kenyon was the officiating judge, he would recommend that the jury ignore Sneyd's monetary hopes in life and award Henry what they thought would recompense his suffering. Quite unexpectedly, though, he reversed his usual position in one of the shortest of his addresses to the jury to appear in print:

> *Gentleman of the Jury*, I have too often had an opportunity of stating to Juries the opinion which I entertain of crimes of this sort. The punishment of them is part of that public duty which the law has reposed in you—I shall only, at present, state to you who the parties are. The plaintiff is a Gentleman of very large property, and the presumptive heir of one of the largest fortunes in the kingdom. His wife also was a Lady of great fortune. The situation of this young man, the defendant, has been intimated to you. This is a subject entirely for your consideration: you will not put him into a situation that will make him a prisoner for life.[44]

Perhaps it was the jury's shock at Kenyon's reversal that led them to come up with damages of just £1,000 after a deliberation of only a few minutes—a measly tenth of the £10,000 Henry had originally asked, rather than the half that juries typically awarded successful plaintiffs in crim con suits.

While this was certainly not the lowest of the damages awarded to wronged husbands in the decades either side of the case, it was certainly low for a man of Henry's rank. Given all the factors that might affect juries' verdicts, it is hard to decide what, precisely, led the jury to award Henry such low damages. Was it Henry's allowing his wife to spend so much time alone with his curate? Was it his bringing his wife to Birmingham? Was it Lord Kenyon's advice to the jury? Or Erskine's ridicule? It could have been any or all of these things: juries do not, after all, give reasons for their decisions, and contemporary accounts did not speculate, laconically recording simply the verdict and damages.[45]

From one perspective, though, the case had been a success. In winning it, Henry was one step closer to obtaining a divorce that would free him from Emma altogether and allow him to remarry Sarah legally. But before he could petition for divorce there was another legal step that needed to be taken.

chapter 6

The Separation

By the time Henry was awarded damages for criminal conversation, the second stage of his divorce proceedings was already well underway. This was an action in the London Consistory Court, an ecclesiastical rather than a civil court, seeking a separation from Emma on the grounds of her adultery.[1] On June 1st, 1790, the Deputy Officer of the court served a citation on Emma Cecil announcing that her husband was suing her for separation. Shortly afterwards, on June 23rd, the Rector of St George, Hanover Square made a copy of the entry of marriage between Henry and Emma to prove that the couple had a valid marriage, a necessary step in the attempt to end it. And the document stating Henry's case against his wife on the grounds of her adultery was presented to the Consistory Court on June 26th, the same day that his crim con suit was presented to the King's Bench.

Fortunately for Henry, immured in pastoral—albeit bigamous—married bliss, he could keep his distance from the Consistory Court in London. Litigants' and deponents' statements were written down by a clerk in response to the questions asked in ecclesiastical litigation. Thus he was able to delegate his case to his proctors and make his statements and provide signatures when necessary in front of a clerk or various legal surrogates. On June 30th, Henry signed the proxy appointing his excellent legal representatives in the ecclesiastical court: Steven Lushington and James Heseltine, Notaries Public and Procurators General of the Arches Court of Canterbury, the diocese in which the London Consistory Court fell.[2]

The London Consistory Court was increasing in popularity as a venue for couples with marital difficulties in the late Georgian period. This was because, conveniently, litigants did not have to be permanently resident in London, but could qualify to sue there after just twenty-one days in residence.[3] Thus both Henry and Emma were recorded as residing at different addresses in the parish of St George, Hanover Square. That Emma was residing there was confirmed by the evidence of the witnesses who identified her. But it seems unlikely that Henry qualified as resident, given what we know about his movements at this time and his absence from the court proceedings. Clearly this was not something that the courts checked too closely.

The court was staffed by expert legal advisors, and suits were fairly rapidly concluded. Sir William Scott, the court's Vicar-General and Chancellor, presided, and, as judge, he personally would decide the outcome of Henry's separation case, rather than a jury as in the crim con suit.

Scott, later Lord Stowell, was an eminent civil-law judge who was extremely influential in matrimonial law.[4] His judgments in cruelty separation cases, for example, led to a major affirmation of the legal definition of cruelty. Presiding over *Evans v Evans* in 1790 he explained that the only acts considered to be cruel were those which were severe enough to make it impossible for a wife to discharge the duties of married life. Famously, he went on: 'What merely wounds the mental feelings is in few cases to be admitted where they are not accompanied with bodily injury, either actual or menaced.'[5] Scholars have claimed that this restated that cruelty constituted life-threatening acts of violence. Yet his mention of 'few cases' and his further declaration that 'apprehension' of hurt should be considered by the ecclesiastical courts 'because assuredly the Court is not to wait till the hurt is actually done,' in actual fact enabled the courts to hear separation cases where violence was less severe.[6]

Scott had strong opinions about adultery, too. He was for example particularly disinclined for ecclesiastical courts to be influenced by previous verdicts in crim con actions, declaring: 'how can that be evidence against the party, which has passed in a suit to which she was not party?'[7] As we have seen, the parties to the crim con action were the husband and alleged lover. The wife was not a party and had no ability to defend herself. In other words, being the adulterous wife in a case of criminal conversation was not of itself direct evidence of adultery that could be set before an ecclesiastical court, and the adultery consequently had to be proved all over again to the satisfaction of this court.

Direct evidence of adultery was very difficult to produce, whatever the court. In ecclesiastical law, two witnesses were required to prove the alleged grounds.[8] This was unlikely to be straightforward; few couples, after all, were incautious enough to be caught *in flagrante*. Other forms of direct evidence might be more feasible to prove, though still problematic, including a wife's confession (but preferably before the court or with witnesses), her pregnancy (as long as it could be proven that her husband was not the father), or her infection with venereal disease.

As a consequence of these difficulties, the ecclesiastical courts allowed circumstantial evidence to be brought. Indeed, many adultery cases called deponents who deposed about peeping through keyholes and cracks in floorboards and door lintels to detect couples in bed, or claimed they heard the creaks of beds and furniture, saw up-turned and crumpled clothing, or washed suspicious stains from bed linen.[9] In 1786, when Sir Martin Stapylton was away at the York Assizes, his wife was spied on by several of his servants. One night their suspicions were aroused when she locked herself in her bedchamber with, they believed, the family's butler. To investigate, the servants gathered around a chink in the door at midnight and saw the bed and its curtains shaking without interruption for a short time and heard 'two persons breathing high and short'. This was cited in Sir Martin's ensuing adultery separation case.[10] When such evidence of sexual congress was not forthcoming, 'vehement presumption, and publick fame' of adultery was valid in separation suits.[11]

In sum, the ecclesiastical courts were prepared to hear evidence of activities that would enable illicit sex to occur. So there were reports of couples alone together for a period of time, particularly when doors were locked, or walking outdoors alone together. Any kissing or touching was of course also considered highly likely to indicate a more intimate sexual relationship.[12] One of the deponents in John Greenwood's 1796 case against his wife deposed that he had seen Mary Greenwood walking in the yard next to his house with Charles Wigglesworth, a local saddler and innkeeper. He noticed that she put one hand behind her back and took hold of Charles' hand, which gave him the 'suspicion that there was something going on betwixt them that ought not to be'.[13]

In many ways the longstanding objective of the ecclesiastical courts was to resolve the marital disharmony that appeared before them, thereby limiting social disorder. They recognized that this was sometimes best achieved by approving a separation. A separation *a mensa et thoro* (literally 'from bed and board') was intended to allow a couple legally to live apart, both giving up their place in the other's bed and at their family table. Although sometimes confusingly termed 'divorces', separations from bed and board were theoretically temporary arrangements, existing until the couple could be reconciled. Separation was permitted on two grounds: cruelty and adultery. It was predominantly husbands who sued their wives on the single ground of adultery in the Georgian era, although wives also accused their husbands of infidelity both as a sole ground, and, more often, as an additional fault to cruelty.[14] The number of adultery separation cases increased in the later eighteenth century, but even so, the numbers of people who could afford this litigation were relatively small.[15] Those men who used them to obtain a divorce in Parliament, by bringing together a separation sentence in their favour from the ecclesiastical courts with an award of damages from a crim con suit in the King's Bench, were fewer still, largely due to the substantial costs involved.[16] Perhaps Henry was, however, expecting his suit to be a comparatively low-cost one, in the cheapest bracket of between £50 and £100 (though still an enormous sum to those outside the aristocracy).[17]

After all, Henry Cecil's adultery suit was relatively simple, as demonstrated by his straightforward 'libel' (as the central document in a separation case was known), which set out in a series of numbered articles the main allegations.[18] Typically, the first three articles of a libel proved the regularity of the union in question. Thus the London Consistory Court was informed that Henry was the only son of the Honourable Thomas Chambers, and Emma the only child and heiress of Thomas Vernon; both their fathers were now deceased. Henry had courted Emma from March to May of 1776, marrying her by licence on May 23rd in the presence of his uncle the Earl of Exeter, Emma's widowed mother, and A.G. Molyneux esquire. The second article offered the proof of the marriage, gathered from the parish book of marriages on June 23rd, and the third article declared that they had consummated the marriage and cohabited together at Hanbury Hall, the seat of Henry Cecil, to the public knowledge of others. The fact that the couple were known to be married by the surrounding community was seen as an important element in confirming that a marriage had in fact taken place in an era before civil registration, when written records of the marriage might well have disappeared even within a relatively short interval.

Henry's case for separation was succinct and focused. The next four articles of the libel named Emma's lover as William Sneyd. They explained that the Rector of Hanbury, the Reverend William Burslem, had engaged the Reverend William Sneyd as a curate in 1783, and that in 1789, without Henry's knowledge, Emma had 'commenced on a very improper and criminal intercourse' with Sneyd.

As in the trial for criminal conversation, Henry's libel endeavoured to show that he had not facilitated his wife's adultery or been aware of her relationship. After all, it was known that Sir William Scott tended to believe that husbands were culpable for their wives' adultery in most cases through neglect, cruelty or adultery.[19] Henry's libel was thus very carefully worded to justify the curate's frequent presence in Hanbury Hall: it was Henry's wealth and liberality that had led to Sneyd being asked to dinner so often.

The description in Henry's libel of Sneyd as becoming one of his 'family' had rather different connotations to eighteenth-century readers. This indication of intimacy was not a statement of equality of status. Masters of households in the eighteenth century routinely referred to their servants, for example, as their 'family'. The term demonstrated a hierarchical relationship between a man and the dependents that were under his care, including those who were not biologically related. This description indicated both Henry's benevolent position at the top of his household's hierarchy, and William Sneyd's access to the household and to Emma, which Sneyd abused by exploiting his role as one of the 'household family'. As such, it placed culpability upon William, not Henry.

In entering a relationship with one of her husband's 'household family', Emma was also guilty of a socially unequal relationship. Although the Sneyds were a land-owning family, and William's father had been in the service of King George III, there was nonetheless a significant status gap between the young gentleman curate and Emma, the heiress. There is no doubt that, had she attempted to marry a man of his rank, parental permission would have been refused.

Many of the adultery separation cases brought in the eighteenth century involved the relationship of a wife with a lover of lower social standing, with some women crossing substantial social gaps. Almost two-thirds of thirty-two cases of adultery in the north of England in the eighteenth century, for example, involved wives unfaithful with men who were of lower station than their husbands, including servants, clerks, and builders.[20] The Reverend Mr William Smith, rector of Ilderton and vicar of Alnham, Northumberland, accused his wife Eleanor in 1789 of adultery with George Fettis, a gardener, and John Smith, a servant. Eleanor, who was in her very early thirties at the time, was presented as an inveterate flirt with men of this station. The rectory had its kitchen rebuilt in summer 1787, and the next year the other end of the house was rebuilt following a fire. Eleanor spent time with the young workmen on both occasions. Her twenty-two-year-old servant Mary Whinham recalled that Eleanor would give them tea and victuals and played at forfeits with them, largely, she suggests, so that she could kiss them. As Mary enumerated, her mistress had kissed the joiner, the plasterer, and the blacksmith....[21]

A further reason for Henry's separation being a relatively simple procedure was that Emma had confessed to her infidelity, eloped with her lover, and was currently living with him—all factors that made her unlikely to mount a defence against the libel's accusations.[22] It is likely that she wanted an end to the marriage just as much as Henry did. But it should nonetheless be noted that it was not uncommon for wives accused of adultery to defend themselves.[23] At its most basic level, the aim of this legal strategy was to establish that they were good wives and fitted the model of an ideal woman: virtuous and honest in character, a competent household manager, and a loving mother.[24] Martin Stapylton's suit, which was heard at the consistory court of Llandaff in 1787, accused his wife Henrietta Maria of being a person of 'loose profligate and adulterous life and conversation'.[25] Henrietta Maria defended herself against the accusations that she had had sex with her father-in-law's coachman and a more sustained relationship with his butler with an allegation that described her as piously brought up and educated, sober, chaste and virtuous, and the victim of her father-in-law, Sir Martin, who disliked his son's marriage to her and insisted that he bring the separation suit against her.[26]

Even if Emma might have had difficulty in claiming such chastity and virtue, she could certainly have pleaded 'recrimination', whereby an accused wife alleged that her husband was also adulterous. This effectively cancelled out the husband's charge and thus his request for separation.[27] If Emma had chosen to do so, she might have been able to track down Henry and discover his adulterous relationship with Sarah Hoggins. Uncovering his bigamy would certainly have stopped his suit, but so would proof that he had simply taken Sarah as his mistress.

But given Emma's relationship with William, her desire to divorce and remarry was as strong as Henry's. She would not be well served in this regard by undermining Henry's suit for separation. This raises the question of whether the suit was collusive. Uncontested suits brought by a husband 'were usually part of a collusive arrangement by which both parties conspired together to prepare the ground for a parliamentary divorce.'[28] If the wife did not contest the suit, then no witnesses would deny the alleged facts. And if both husband and wife sought an end to their marriage, they could 'conceal, invent, or create facts' to ensure their separation was successful and thereby facilitate a parliamentary divorce. Another form of collusion involved bringing a defence but producing witnesses who actually offered proof of the infidelity.[29] While there is no evidence that the Cecils colluded to manufacture or distort evidence, there were certain facts that neither would have wished to bring forward.[30]

And a close comparison with Henry's letters to William Burslem exposes how far the separation documents lodged with the London Consistory Court were tactical accounts rather than truthful narratives of events. Guided no doubt by his own or by Burslem's discussions with advocates or proctors, Henry disclosed to the Consistory Court very little about the events of his marital breakdown. His strategy was clear: avoid any risk of being accused of conniving in or condoning Emma's relationship by allowing her to stay in the marital home or, worse, the marital bed once he had had knowledge of her adultery. The libel thus twice affirmed that Henry 'never lived or cohabited' (a euphemism for having sexual relations) with Emma after she eloped from him on June 12th, 1789.

Emphasising that he had never tolerated the adulterous relationship was even more important in the ecclesiastical courts than in the civil courts. In the latter, when suing for criminal conversation, evidence that the husband had connived at the affair might well reduce the damages payable to him, but it did not prevent him succeeding in his action. But in the ecclesiastical courts, the charge of connivance in a wife's affair meant that a husband knew about her infidelity but allowed it to continue, proof of which was a bar to the separation suit succeeding. Henry's correspondence with Burslem reveals he needed to be cautious in this respect. Writing in September of 1789, he reported that Emma had confessed to being attached to Sneyd for five years. While it is unclear from the evidence when the affair actually began, Emma, had she wanted to preserve her status as his wife, could well have argued that Henry could not have been unaware of her love for another man over several years.[31]

Henry's libel also never mentioned Emma's confession. This is because he had not turned Emma out of Hanbury Hall immediately on discovering her infidelity. Indeed, as he told Burslem a few months later, 'So dreadfully agitated was her mind and body that, I believe, my sole business was to prevent, as I thought, an immediate dissolution; for in truth I did not give credit to all she said, nor could I give up my opinion of her so suddenly'. He wisely added, however, that 'She has never slept in my bed from the time [William Sneyd] was first taken ill', for he needed to avoid the charge of condoning Emma's adultery.

Emma could have used such a charge against Henry had she been determined to remain in the marriage. Condonation meant that a wronged spouse had forgiven the adultery and that the couple were reconciled, indicated by them allowing the offending spouse back into the marital home and bed. In fact, sleeping together after learning of the adultery implied the husband's acceptance of his wife's infidelity, and is the reason why most adultery libels stated that the husband had turned out his unfaithful wife as soon as he was made aware of her offending behaviour.[32] In 1776, John Taylor, a Bridlington attorney, sued his wife for adultery and claimed that when he discovered she had been adulterous, he 'totally refrained from laying with her... and never since had the carnal love or knowledge of her body'.[33] This was no small detail: if an accused wife could prove condonation, she could succeed in having her husband's suit for separation barred from court.[34] Besides, a husband who lost his case due to condonation was prevented from trying to obtain a parliamentary divorce, and remained financially responsible for his wife during—and even after—his lifetime.[35]

Other precautions that Henry took are apparent in the gap between his report of events to Burslem and his libel as presented to the court. In his communication with Burslem in September of 1789, Henry admitted he was deeply distressed by the news of his wife's betrayal three months before and not keen to end the relationship immediately. It was not until he had gone to Lichfield to get confirmation of Emma's dramatic declaration that he accepted the 'fatal truth.' Even so, he returned to Hanbury determined not to aggravate Emma's misfortunes but to 'do every thing in my power, that she wished, consistent with my Honor, to alleviate her sufferings.' He told Burslem that 'I did everything in my power to persuade her to alter her determination', telling her that he would continue to live with her and conceal her misfortune if she would give up Sneyd. He even offered that, if she broke up with her lover, 'I would take upon myself the cause of our separation and would conceal the reasons'.

These were noble sentiments, particularly since they had no surviving children to protect from their mother's public loss of reputation. But such statements, together with Henry's kindness in permitting Emma to see Sneyd once more and in accompanying her to Birmingham, might well have posed problems in his separation suit.

By the summer of 1790, newly (if bigamously) married, Henry needed to win his case with the least enquiry possible into the affair or its aftermath. Thus the libel entirely removed reference to Emma's confession, simply stating that at the end of May William was taken ill at Hanbury Hall and was removed to recover at his father's house at Lichfield. In June, the libel went on, Henry and Emma agreed to make an 'excursion' to Birmingham, along with another 'lady' (presumably the less said about the lady being Sneyd's brother's wife the better, since such complex family webs would only complicate matters further). They arrived at the hotel on June 12th, 1789, and while Henry was employed in some business in town, Emma 'quitted and left' the hotel to meet Sneyd, for, 'by some means unknown' to Henry, she had contrived to acquaint her lover with her arrival at Birmingham. Henry's involvement in the elopement was therefore also erased.

The libel focused instead on the eloped pair's perambulations around the south west of England using fictitious names and disguises, with Sneyd wearing different coloured clothes and dressing his hair to disguise his professional status as a clergyman. The remaining articles explained that they arrived in Exeter on June 18th and stayed at Thompson's Hotel until the 22nd, moved to lodge at Richard During's house at Dawlish in the county of Devon for seven weeks, and then went to the Blue Bell Inn at Bruton in Somerset for a fortnight.[36]

At the start of September, however, Emma and William separated for eight months, she to London, he to Ireland. No explanation was given in the libel for this parting, but it is likely that William went to stay with his sister Elizabeth, who was then living at Edgeworthstown in County Longford, where her husband Richard Lovell Edgeworth's family estate was situated. Money would have been tight for William—who had lost his stipend upon his elopement—and it would have been galling for him to be supported by Emma.

The two lovers were apart until Easter of 1790, when William returned from Ireland to lodge with Emma, who now lived at 19, New Norfolk Street (now Dunraven Street, lying just behind London's Park Lane). Until their temporary time apart they had called themselves 'Mr and Mrs Benson', and in all places, as the libel declared, Emma had committed the 'foul sin of adultery'.

The profile of the deponents brought to give evidence to the Consistory Court was unusual, since most adultery cases with spouses of high social standing called upon the servants of the marital household to recall activities and events that proved their mistresses' adultery.[37] Around a third of the deponents called in Roger Manwaring's suit against his wife, for example, were servants.[38] In Henry's suit, however, only one deponent was a household servant: William Jauncey, the thirty-seven-year-old servant who had featured so heavily in the trial for criminal conversation. He was interviewed by the Consistory Court much later, on January 3rd, 1791. Jauncey established that he had worked at Hanbury Hall in Henry's service since 1785 and knew the Cecils well, thus confirming their public status as a married couple. Sneyd, he explained, was often backwards and forwards at Hanbury Hall, although true to his firmness as a witness in Henry's crim con suit in July of 1790, he claimed he did not know if Emma had committed adultery with him. Jauncey also deposed that Henry had returned alone to Hanbury on June 12th, and that Henry had been there occasionally, after leaving in July of 1789, until November, but that he had not seen Henry anywhere else.

Most of the other deponents were people who came into contact with Emma and William *after* they had eloped; their purpose was to prove Emma's adultery following her elopement. Three such deponents were interviewed on July 5th, 1790. Ann Winnicombe, a forty-year-old upper chambermaid at Thompson's Hotel in Exeter, deposed that in June of 1789 a coach with black horses had arrived carrying a lady and gentleman; he wore a 'pepper and salt coloured coat' and his hair was tied behind so that he did not resemble a clergyman. She remembered that the couple slept in the same room because she had to pin a blanket over the window curtain, since the pernickety lady declared she could not sleep where there was the least light.[39] Sarah During, the forty-year-old wife of the landlord Richard During, of Dawlish in Devon, recalled that on June 19th a couple had arrived from Exeter and taken apartments in her house for three months (a parlour and kitchen on the ground floor, a bedroom over the kitchen, and a dressing room and two bedrooms on the second floor). Elizabeth Cross, a nineteen-year-old unmarried chambermaid at the Blue Bell Inn in Bruton, recalled that early in August of 1789, on a Sunday, a lady and gentleman and a maid had arrived in a post-chaise, with a manservant on horseback. They had stayed for a fortnight. None of the women saw the couple in bed together. However, Ann, who cared for the linen in the hotel, claimed that the bed looked slept in by two people, and said she had seen Mr Benson leave the room in his morning gown. Sarah noted that the couple only had one bedroom and both kept their clothes in it. And Elizabeth said that she had frequently seen the lady in the bed and the gentleman locking the door so that they were alone together in the room. All agreed that the couple called themselves Mr and Mrs Benson and employed a manservant and a maid.

Henry was obviously prepared to go to considerable effort and money in order to establish that the couple known as the Bensons were the same man and woman now residing in London. The three women all confirmed that in mid June they and William Jauncey were brought to London to confirm that the Bensons, who had visited their various hotel, lodgings, and inn, were the same people now living in New Norfolk Street as Emma Cecil and William Sneyd. The group was probably ensconced in the inn, The City of Norwich Arms, opposite William and Emma's house, which, along with the expenses they were granted, must have made the trip to London less onerous. They saw a lady come to the window of 19, New Norfolk Street, and the women confirmed that she was Mrs Benson, while Jauncey confirmed that this was Emma Cecil. The following Monday, the same group of witnesses went to a house in Green Street, which adjoined New Norfolk Street, and there saw William Sneyd at a window, wearing a dressing gown. They waited in the street for some time, until Sneyd left the house and visited 19, New Norfolk Street. Again Jauncey confirmed Sneyd's identity for his fellow witnesses, who identified him as Mr Benson.[40] A further three deponents were interviewed on January 31st, all of whom confirmed that Emma Cecil lived in New Norfolk Street and was visited by William Sneyd. A sedan-bearer from nearby Grosvenor Square explained that he delivered letters between Emma and William and had seen William visit Emma while sitting in the inn opposite. James Bursnoll and Elizabeth Sky, the son of the master of the City of Norwich Arms and an eighteen-year-old servant, also confirmed seeing William visiting, and sending beer and ale over to Emma's lodgings, delivering to her under the name Cecil.

The final deponent was Henry's uncle, the sixty-five-year-old Brownlow, Earl of Exeter. As well as confirming various details about the Cecils' marriage, he alluded to the rift between him and his nephew, explaining that the Cecils had been planning to visit him at Burghley in June of 1789 in order to attend the races at Stamford. In the week of the races however he had been 'greatly surprized' to receive a letter from Henry, who told him that Emma had eloped. Since then, he said he had seen neither party.

The rupture between Brownlow and Henry emerged more clearly in Henry's correspondence with Burslem. A letter in April of 1790 denied responsibility for the estrangement. Indeed, Henry declared that, losing his uncle's confidence and affection after his wife's elopement, he felt 'the greatest ties of social intercourse being sever'd by the conduct of the two persons who were nearest to me in blood and affections'.

No doubt another reason for Henry's misery was, as we have seen, that he was uneasy that his uncle would use his nephew's attempt to get a divorce as a way to avoid leaving him Burghley House after his death.[41]

Despite the potential obstacles, and Henry's occasional worries about what the impact of the divorce might be, his legal tactics were successful, and, along with the clear proof that Emma and William had continued to commit adultery together after June 12th, 1790, persuaded the judge to decide in Henry's favour.

But there was one final thing that needed to be done to conclude the proceedings. Henry needed to appear in person and swear that he would abide by the conditions of the separation order. Even at this point in the litigation, Henry did not leave his cottage in Great Bolas and return to London. Instead, the London Consistory Court issued letters of request to the Bishop of Worcester that he take Henry's bond to this effect, and on February 15th Henry duly appeared before the bishop's surrogate and promised that he would not marry any other person while Emma was still alive. By this period, of course, those involved in the granting of separation orders would have known that this was something of a hollow promise, and that the order was being obtained as a preliminary to a divorce. Nonetheless, the terms of the order maintained the fiction that separation was all that was intended.[42] The bond was executed on February 27th, and the sentence was read and promulgated in court four days later. Henry was now formally separated from Emma. By gaining this separation 'from bed and board', his risky game had succeeded. Had it been known that he had committed bigamy, though, he would inevitably have failed. He was now another step closer to obtaining the parliamentary divorce that would enable him to remarry.

chapter 7

The Divorce

The terms of the separation handed down by the London Consistory Court required that neither Henry nor Emma remarry while the other was still alive, and only a Parliamentary divorce would countermand that requirement and allow the two to wed Sarah and William. To this end, divorce acts included a clause that specifically allowed the soon-to-be-divorced spouses to marry once more. In the rather cumbersome language used in divorce bills, Henry's clause requested that his marriage

> be and is hereby and henceforth wholly dissolved annulled vacated and made void to all intents purposes and constructions whatsoever and that it shall and may be lawful to and for the said Henry Cecil at any time or times hereafter to contract matrimony and to marry as well in the life time of the said Emma Cecil as if she was actually dead.[1]

But Henry was by no means guaranteed that Parliament would grant him a private divorce. He certainly could not have obtained a divorce had he lost his criminal conversation trial or his case at the London Consistory Court, because Parliament required men seeking divorces (and it was always men, no woman having yet sought to avail herself of the procedure) to have won both cases. But winning both trials did not in itself assure Henry of his divorce, because Parliament did not feel bound by the decisions of those lower courts. So, what did Henry have to do to succeed in this last step to complete his split from Emma?

From the perspective of the twenty-first century, where the divorce process is relatively straightforward, the legal issues to be overcome in the late eighteenth century were complex. Henry's first step was to file a petition, stating that he was seeking a divorce on the grounds of Emma's adultery. Henry took this step on March 2nd, 1791, the very same day his case in the London Consistory Court was decided in his favour. He must in fact have had the petition prepared ahead of time, ready to be presented to Parliament almost the minute the Consistory Court had handed down its decision.

Once Parliament approved the petition, Henry then had to submit a bill made up of a set of standard clauses, a step he took the day following that on which his petition was approved. Such a bill did not provide details of how or why the adultery took place—there could be no reference here to Sneyd's frequent presence at their house, to Emma's confession of her adultery, to the trip to Birmingham that led to her elopement with Sneyd, nor to their behaviour thereafter. The clause that asked that the marriage be 'dissolved annulled vacated and made void' was standard to divorce bills, although it typically came late in them. Other clauses set forth when the couple married, when the adultery occurred, and when the husband stopped cohabiting with his wife. Ideally, from the law's point of view, he had ceased living with his wife on the day he discovered the adultery, the better to stress that he had never countenanced it, but these clauses typically only gave the month and year of both the start of the adultery and the cessation of cohabitation. So Henry's bill simply stated that the adultery had started in June of 1790, and that he had neither lived with nor had contact with Emma since that month.

Sometimes these bills also set forth the wife's marriage portion and marriage settlement, the latter of which could be quite lengthy if the couple had extensive property, as it was in Henry and Emma's case. In fact, in Henry's divorce bill—at twenty-four pages, it was quite a bit longer than most—description of the settlements ran from the second through to the twelfth page.

Once the bill was submitted, it was read to Parliament three times. The first reading was a brief affair that simply acquainted MPs with the bill's content and decided when the second reading would take place. Naming at this early stage the date of the second reading then gave those who needed to be present at this trial—Henry and Emma, their counsels, and their witnesses—time to come to Parliament. These witnesses would typically be the same witnesses who had appeared at the criminal conversation trial, and who had deposed in the London Consistory Court, with perhaps the addition of some others. This trial would take place first and most extensively before the House of Lords, though witnesses could also be questioned and counsel heard before the House of Commons as well.[2]

The purpose of this investigation was to prove once again (this time to Parliament's satisfaction) that adultery had in fact occurred. Parliament was also required to consider, as had the London Consistory Court, 'whether there has or has not been any collusion, directly or indirectly on [Henry's] part, ...or whether there be any collusion, directly or indirectly, between him and his wife, or any other person or persons.'[3] Henry and Emma were obliged to appear in person, since Parliament might have wanted to question them on the issue of collusion. But, as in the trials they had already gone through in the common-law and ecclesiastical courts, neither were called upon to testify. Instead, the barristers representing each of them presented their cases and questioned and cross-examined witnesses, while MPs interjected with their own questions. With Mr Graham representing Emma and Mr Bower representing Henry, the Cecil trial took place on April 8th, 1791, about two weeks after the bill was first read.

Very occasionally in such proceedings, one of the principal players might be examined in person, as was the wife's lover in one case some eight years later. This was the utterly scandalous case in which Charles Collins Campbell sought to divorce his wife Harriet, who had had an affair with her uncle, Major Archibald Hook. Campbell had gone to India to join his regiment and left his wife under the protection of her mother; Hook had assumed guardianship and ultimately seduced Harriet. Hook, wanting to clear his name, desired to be heard during the Parliamentary trial and swore vehemently that he had 'never taken any Liberty that a Person situated as [he] was, had not a complete Right to with his Niece.'[4] But witness testimony about the tumbled and stained state of Harriet's sheets undermined his assertions, while another servant, who had spied on them through a keyhole to Harriet's bedroom, claimed to have seen Hook stark naked in his niece's bedroom.[5] Some servants contradicted these assertions, as did Hook himself, but their claims were not found convincing. Members of Parliament hearing the case may also have been influenced by the testimony of one witness in the lower courts that Hook had been overheard telling his niece she was 'the worst of whores'—and her replying that 'I own that I am a whore to you, and to you only.'[6]

Bigamy might have vied with incest as the most shocking thing that could be revealed in cases of marital breakdown, but, fortunately for Henry, there was little reason for Parliament even to suspect that he had committed bigamy when in March of 1791 he started the process of divorcing Emma. If it were to be revealed that he had married Sarah Hoggins eleven months earlier, Henry's chances of obtaining a divorce would inevitably have ended in defeat and scandal.

Much of what happened in Parliament repeated the steps taken in the lower courts. First, Henry and Emma's marriage had to be proved by producing a copy of the church register in which it had been recorded. Typically, witnesses to the wedding would also be called on to verify that it had taken place and to identify the parties as those involved in the case. Next, copies of the decisions in the criminal conversation trial and in the London Consistory Court had to be produced. Then came witness testimony that the adultery had occurred. Ann Winnicombe once against testified that Emma and William had stayed at Thomson's Hotel and that they had slept in the same bed. Again she stated that when in London with Sarah During, Elizabeth Cross, and William Jauncey, she saw Emma, whom she identified as 'Mrs Benson', and that Jauncey had told her who 'Mrs Benson' really was.[7] Sarah said that with these other three, she had identified 'Mr Benson', but again, William Jauncey had identified the man for who he really was. Jauncey himself then testified to the same end.[8]

An additional and very important witness was also questioned. The testimony of Maria Sneyd, William's sister-in-law, who had gone to Birmingham with Emma and Henry, was particularly interesting because it did not corroborate earlier suggestions that Henry had allowed Emma to go to Birmingham 'on a party of pleasure'.[9] By this point, the Lords had learned that Emma had confessed her adultery to her husband, and many of the questions Maria was asked attempted to establish whether or not Henry and Emma, or possibly even William as well, had colluded to present a case based on Emma's adultery, or whether or not Henry had condoned it. Thus they asked her directly: 'Mrs Cecil having made a confession of her guilt, did Mr and Mrs Cecil separate?' Maria had to admit that they did not separate immediately, which risked giving the impression that Henry had condoned the adultery. Nonetheless, she emphasised that the two had slept separately, with she herself in fact sleeping in the same room as the now openly adulterous Emma. Maria was also questioned about Sneyd's frequent residence at Hanbury Hall, which might have suggested, once again, that Henry had condoned his wife's relationship with the curate. Maria stated that Sneyd occasionally slept at Hanbury Hall, but that he certainly was not in the house when Emma confessed, nor afterwards.[10]

Just why Maria was asked in so many different ways whether Henry had colluded in the adultery for the sake of getting a divorce might have had something to do with who the Lord Chancellor was when the bill was being heard. As one historian has pointed out, while a large number of Lords might attend when divorce bills were discussed, 'the Chancellor was usually the only lawyer present, and as such the only person who could conduct a sustained cross-examination of the witnesses.' He analysed the success rate of divorce bills brought to Parliament from the 1780s to the 1820s and concluded that the three Lord Chancellors during that time—Lords Thurlow, Loughborough, and Eldon—'all disliked divorce and thought that it tended to collusion. But only [Lords] Thurlow and Eldon habitually acted as chief inquisitor.'[11] And it was Lord Thurlow who was Lord Chancellor when Henry's case came to Parliament.

Lord Thurlow in 1784

Henry's was clearly a difficult case, with suspicions that something lay behind the facts as stated to Parliament, but it lacked the sorts of specific allegations of condonation or collusion that emerged in other cases heard around the same time. It can be contrasted with the particularly egregious case of Lord Valentia, who wanted to divorce his wife Lady Ann for adultery with John Bellenden Gawler and who petitioned Parliament to this end in 1799. Condonation or levity—a lack of concern for a wife's adultery—had already become clear in the crim con trial. Lord Valentia wanted children so that the next in line for his estate would not inherit; so long as his wife bore children, he didn't care who the actual father was, and he had said before a number of people that 'he did not care if the Devil got them.'[12] In fact, when his wife became pregnant with a second child, after having previously had a son, Valentia was reported to have told Gawler, 'Jack, I do not know whose child this will be—but I know the last was your's.'[13] Because the adultery could be proven, Valentia won his crim con suit and then his separation from bed and board at the ecclesiastical courts, but simply winning these trials did not guarantee that Valentia would be granted a Parliamentary divorce. He ultimately withdrew his bill, saying that key witnesses could not attend, but, given his actions in condoning his wife's adultery, he must have known he had little chance that his bill would pass muster in Parliament.

Another man, Andrew Bayntun, had eventually succeeded in obtaining a parliamentary divorce, but only after evidence was brought forward to counter potentially damaging allegations of collusion. In 1783, one witness claimed that Bayntun had asked his wife's lover to 'go to bed to his Wife, and permit Witnesses to see them in that Situation.'[14] Before Parliament this witness was even more explicit, claiming that after Bayntun learned of the adultery, he said to his wife's lover, 'I have [a] favour to beg of you, Jack, that you will go to bed with Lady Maria and allow some of my Servants to come in and see you in that Situation, in order that I may obtain my Divorce with as little Trouble and Expence as possible.'[15] Happily for Andrew, one of his brothers, the Reverend Henry Bayntun, contradicted these allegations and emphasised Andrew's distress when Maria handed back her wedding ring.[16] Parliament eventually decided that there had not been collusion between the parties and allowed the bill to pass. But in the decades either side of Cecil's case no fewer than four men found guilty of collusion had their bills rejected.[17]

So it was clearly a very real risk. If Parliament felt that Henry was guilty of collusion or levity he would lose his chance of a divorce. It is true that his behaviour to Emma after she confessed to adultery could not compete with Lord Valentia's for obvious and egregious condonation, but the Lords were still suspicious of the fact that Henry had apparently delivered Emma into her lover's hands. When Maria Sneyd told the Lords that Emma had first confessed the adultery to Henry and later to her, they wondered whether Cecil was as calm or indeed as happy as Bayntun was represented (at least by one witness) to have been. Maria told them, however, that Henry 'was extremely distressed with it'. On being asked 'But he did not think of parting with her?'—a question that might today be considered as leading the witness—she answered 'Not immediately, the first time I believe.'[18] Was this admitting that Henry had later thought with equanimity of parting with Emma? That he perhaps would not actually have minded her eloping with Sneyd? That he had in fact *intended* to deliver her to Sneyd?

Maria's further testimony emphasised, however, that Henry was innocent of even an inkling of collusion. She asserted that 'Mrs Cecil declared she would not give up Mr Sneyd unless she was permitted to see him'; that this was 'the first thing [Emma] said to her husband,' and that Henry had objected to it—at least at first. And, she went on, he only gave in because Emma had 'urged him so strongly, that he consented to it from seeing her so distracted'. The evidence as to Emma's mental state was suitably dramatic:

> She was not in her senses at the time.... She appeared extremely agitated, and she threatened to destroy herself. ... She threatened to destroy herself that evening.

What could a husband do in this position? 'He felt himself obliged to let her go,' Maria added.[19] But she could not disguise the fact that it took another two weeks before Emma left, which could have suggested either that Henry was reasoning with her, hoping she would change her mind, or that he was unconcerned. Then more facts came out. Maria told their Lordships that Emma had asked her to accompany her and Henry to the rendezvous in Birmingham and that Emma had voluntarily promised to return to Hanbury after a final adieu to Sneyd.[20] Another Lord then questioned Maria, asking whether Henry 'was indifferent about it'—clearly doubts still remained as to whether or not he had cared that Emma was having an affair with Sneyd. Maria refused to substantiate such an idea, however, answering, indignantly perhaps, that she did not know this to be true.[21] On being asked whether any steps had been taken 'to persuade Mrs Cecil to break off her [adulterous] connection,' Maria replied that Henry had proposed a number of alternatives—either that they would remain together at Hanbury Hall, or that they would leave it together and go to some distant part of England for a while, or even that they would separate, with Henry, like a gentleman, appearing to be the guilty party—but all on the proviso that Emma gave up William.[22] All this worked in Henry's favour, since it emphasised that he did not countenance the adulterous connection continuing. But Maria unfortunately revealed another fact: apparently, Emma did not actually 'consent to give [William] up' after seeing him.[23] This risked suggesting to their Lordships that a different construction could be put on the trip to Birmingham: it was one thing to permit a distracted and near-suicidal wife a final meeting with her lover as a condition of her giving him up forever. It was quite another to arrange such a meeting when she had not agreed to any such condition.

Reading Maria Sneyd's testimony, we also get a clearer picture of what transpired in Birmingham. Maria and Emma went to the Hen and Chickens, the hotel where William was staying. Her husband Edward—William's brother—had arrived there with William, and he and Maria retreated to a room (or at least a passage) adjoining that in which Emma was supposedly parting with William. After an hour, Maria and her husband 'went into a shop very near' for 'about another hour', but, as one of the Lords asked, 'At the end of that time you found they were gone?' All Maria could say was a simple 'yes'. She did affirm, however, that Henry was so thunderstruck that he apparently could not speak at first, and appeared very dismayed.[24]

After hearing all this evidence, were the Lords convinced that there had been no collusion, no condonation, no levity on Henry's part? Had the topic been put to bed, so to speak? When they reconvened on May 4th and discussed the case among themselves, they brought up these issues more explicitly. The Lord Chancellor, Edward Thurlow, argued that Henry's consent for Emma to see William one last time and his permitting her 'to go alone to the adulterer'[25] had 'much the air of indifference about the morals of his lady; there was too much levity in it. It was at the very best, incautious and unbecoming behaviour'. He believed that none of the main players could prove that there had been no collusion—or at least that they had not proved this satisfactorily.

Henry's future hung in the balance. But eventually, after 'conversing with those better acquainted with the nature of those matters,' Lord Thurlow decided not to oppose the second reading of the bill.[26] He may have been moved to this position by Lord Coventry's assertion that Henry's allowing Emma to meet William was 'wholly to be ascribed to an error of judgment.'[27] Henry could not have known that Maria and her husband would have left the erring couple alone for an hour—more than enough time for them to elope. At least, this is the story that the Lords finally accepted.

Next, there was the little matter of how Emma was to survive after the divorce. Looking solely at the divorce bills of the time, one might form the impression that husbands did not have to pay their ex-wives alimony. If they did not, adulterous wives would indeed be in dire straits. If their lovers did not marry them—and some could not, being already married themselves—these women would potentially have had a very hard time finding another husband, and, if they could not, they may have had to hope that their own families would support them.

But there was no guarantee that an ex-wife would be granted any support from her ex-husband after a divorce. In one case in 1783, the same Lord Thurlow had acknowledged, no doubt with disgust, that

> it was the practice of that House, when an injured husband applied for relief, and a bill of divorce *a vincula matrimonii* passed, that a sort of composition took place, and the husband was called upon to pay an annuity to the wife, on account of the recovery of his freedom.[28]

So it had been the practice of Parliament to order men to provide at least some financial support for their ex-wives. Yet Thurlow nonetheless went on to stress his opinion that

> It was contrary to law, and indeed it was opposite to justice. What! pay a woman for adultery! Provide for her because she is infamous! It must not be. The law is, that when she becomes an adultress, and is discovered, she forfeits her claim to alimony. Is the legislature in such a case to interpose, and, because the guilt is fully proved, make a recompence to the Lady, for the prostitution of which she has been found guilty? No: that would be absurdity to the highest degree. The divorce is meant as a punishment; and the only way to make that punishment operate, is not to make any pecuniary provision for the culprit.[29]

Not all took such a harsh view, though, and some husbands—perhaps not wishing to see their ex-wives in the gutter—did provide financial support. Sometimes the amount was stated explicitly in the bill, sometimes allusion was made to the fact that provision had been made, but not the sum,[30] and sometimes we learn of it solely through the debates in Parliament.[31] One way in which it might come to be discussed was if the wife being divorced felt that the provision made for her was inadequate and petitioned Parliament to reconsider it.[32] Some of these petitions read as simply as Lady Elizabeth Vassall's, which stated that 'if the said [divorce] Bill shall pass into a Law as it now stands, it would greatly affect your petitioner'.[33] Even more plaintively, another soon-to-be-divorced wife, the Right Honourable Lady Elizabeth Belasyse, wrote in 1794 that 'if the [bill] shall pass into a Law as it now stands your petitioner will be deprived of all her said Fortune and left intirely destitute.' She pointed out that this was all the more unfair in that 'the Fortune of your Petitioner at the time of the said marriage amounted to £12,600.'[34]

Emma was equally aggrieved by the financial provision that was being proposed for her. True, she would not be left destitute: while the bill did not state it overtly, there was a provision made of £500 per year, and she was also receiving interest from money that had been invested in the public funds. The sums in question were somewhere between £14,000 and £18,000—the newspapers that published accounts of the debates in Parliament reported widely differing amounts, even when the men taking down the proceedings in shorthand had attended the same session and heard exactly the same numbers bandied about. And a sum of money left to her by her aunt Annabella Cornwall—her mother's sister, who had died in 1782—also generated a certain amount of income.[35]

But Emma clearly felt that she had the right to expect rather more: she had, after all, brought an even larger fortune to her marriage than Lady Elizabeth Belasyse. In her petition to Parliament asking for financial provision to be made for her, she noted that 'Henry Cecil on his Marriage with your Petitioner became intitled to a very large Estate and Fortune of your Petitioner the whole of which is by certain Clauses in the said Bill taken away from her without any Provision being made for her support or Maintenance of the same.' Her point was not that she was left with nothing, but simply that Henry proposed keeping everything that he had gained from the marriage, while she was to lose even the pin money of £1,000 per year that had been provided by the Earl of Exeter.

In addition, Emma was all the more upset by the fact that Henry's divorce bill, if passed into law as it stood, 'would vest in the said Henry Cecil certain powers over the said Estate which might be prejudicial to the persons claiming next after your Petitioner in Remainder or Reversion'.[36] In other words, since Henry only had a life interest in his soon-to-be-ex-wife's estate, and would not be able to pass it on to any children he might have, he had no incentive to maintain it for the next generation. As Sir John Ingilby pointed out, when the bill went to the House of Commons, Henry had already had the parks ploughed up and trees cut down, and was using the estate to pay off his creditors.[37] This second problem turned out to be the easier of the two to fix: the Lords added a clause to Henry's divorce bill stating that 'it shall not be lawful for the said Henry Cecil or his assigns to cut down any timber or other trees within the Park called Hanbury Park,' thereby protecting the property for whomever would inherit it after Henry's death.[38]

But the issue of what monies Emma was to retain from her original fortune or her marriage settlements sparked heated debate. Her counsel asked that she receive £1,000, the amount of her pin money. This would mean, however, that she had precisely the same fortune for herself that she had had during her marriage; the only difference would be that such things as a home and food would not be covered by anyone else. Henry's counsel, Mr Bower, thought that Emma's retaining such a fortune was improper, hoping that the Lords would 'not consider a person so guilty entitled to that provision and those comforts she would have enjoyed by continuing in the path of virtue.' He added that the fortune had in any event been 'assigned over for the benefit of [Henry's] creditors' — we must remember that either he, or both he and Emma, had spent well beyond their annual income—so Henry was simply not able to promise to pay her £1,000 from the estate. Furthermore, Mr Bower pointed out, 'as she was entitled to the reversion of between fourteen and fifteen thousand pounds he must hope their Lordships would not place guilt in a superior situation to that of innocence.'[39]

Emma did have some sympathy among the Lords. Lord Coventry, whose daughter Maria had been divorced by Andrew Bayntun a few years earlier, objected to leaving the bill in its original form 'upon the ground that, highly offensive as the crime of adultery was, he knew of no law that annexed the confiscation of property as part of the punishment.'[40] But the Lord Chancellor vigorously argued in response that, while there was no such law, 'yet it was the principle upon which that House had acted for a great length of time',[41] reminding them that 'the Law of Parliament did not hold out rewards instead of punishment to the Adulteress.'[42]

So it was unsurprising that the bill was accepted by their Lordships as it stood. On May 11th it was sent to committee, which made 'a few slender amendments.'[43] These were then presented to the House of Lords on May 19th, including the clause protecting the trees of Hanbury Park. The Lords then passed the bill the next day and sent it to the House of Commons.

Here, however, there were more vocal, determined, and high-profile men willing to champion Emma's cause—and that of divorced wives in general. As discussion of the bill continued in early June, the issue of Emma's alimony appears to have been the primary issue with which the House of Commons was concerned. Chief among them was Charles James Fox, supporter of liberty, religious tolerance and the French Revolution, perennially in opposition, and with a notorious private life of his own. He, Mr Taylor, and Mr Baker all agreed that 'in all bills of this sort, a provision should be made for the wife, whether she had a fortune or not.'[44] Fox added that 'it was unreasonable and outrageous that a man who was obliged to support his wife by the law of the land, should by an application to Parliament be completely relieved from that burden, without any consideration; it was not... consistent with justice.'[45] Furthermore, Fox felt that 'there ought to be an allowance that would enable the unhappy women who had fallen into such faults, to live in a decent and becoming manner, as it might prevent them from falling into a course that would cut off hopes of contrition.'[46] To his mind, Parliament's goal was to help the erring wife to repent rather than to punish her. As Charles Fox's remarks suggested, he wanted a rule put in place that would guarantee *all* women being divorced to have some kind of decent provision. He argued that just as a woman was granted a provision after a judicial separation, she should also be provided such support after a parliamentary divorce.[47]

In Henry and Emma's case, Parliament did not need to continue the argument; agents for both Henry and Emma told the House of Commons that the Earl of Exeter had now promised to continue to provide Emma with the £1,000 that she had previously had as pin money. With the various other sums to which she was entitled, she would have a fairly substantial income, even if part of it were dependent on the goodwill of her former in-laws rather than a binding legal commitment.[48]

Emma's accepting Lord Exeter's provision should have meant an end to wrangling over the issue in the House of Commons. But it instead led back to the issue of collusion. Did the fact that financial provision had been agreed behind the scenes mean that the couple were colluding to present the divorce case and obtain their freedom from each other? As Sir William Scott explained, 'consent of parties... was always a circumstance of suspicion in [divorce] cases... and ought to operate rather as an alarm to the caution of the house, than as a circumstance tending to satisfy them that their duty was performed' in granting the couple a divorce.[49]

In the event, though, the Commons gave the parties the benefit of the doubt. While noting that 'it was… their duty to prevent any thing that looked like collusion,' Sir William said that any such suspicions were no doubt due to the bill's having been 'not so well explained as it ought to have been.'[50] Another MP supported Sir William's conclusion, saying that because there were no 'circumstances… in proof before the House' that there was collusion, 'it should not affect the Bill in its present stage.'[51] The fact that the Lords had already considered the issue of collusion and decided that this was not a case where this was a problem no doubt influenced this conclusion.

The main concern that remained, then, was whether the provision for Emma should have been included within the bill itself or just left as an informal agreement. In part because the latter path was taken, about a third of the House of Commons voted against the bill. Even so, it passed with a vote of forty-eight in favour of the bill and twenty-four against. On June 10th, only about two-and-a-half months after Henry had petitioned for his divorce, King George III gave the bill his Royal Assent. Once the bill became a private Act, Henry was, in the eyes of Parliament and the king, a single man.

chapter 8

Reconciliation & Remarriage

The divorce having finally been granted, Henry travelled to London and was reconciled with his uncle Brownlow. In August he wrote to the Reverend Burslem to tell him that:

> The meeting in [Lower] Grosvenor St this morning at 10'o clock was very affecting; the Peer cried, but recovered soon. Then talked of business and of himself.... He asked how long I would stay; on my saying a few days, he said, do as you please, but let your friends see you now and then. He seems not willing that I should not be with him long at a time, but wishes to see me at stated times.[1]

But then Brownlow, who is said to have 'enjoyed' ill-health, seems by this time to have had real cause for concern. He was in London to be examined by a surgeon, but planned to leave as soon as he could: Henry reported him as saying that 'if I am to expect to die now, it shall be at home.' And perhaps he had hoped for a longer visit from the nephew who had disappeared without notice, and whom he had not seen for so long. Henry, however, was eager to return to Shropshire, and to Sarah. At the same time as he was writing to Burslem, he was also penning a short but heartfelt note to her:

> Dear Sally, My heart aches sadly at being kept so long from you; as I have no happiness in this world but with you, you may judge how miserable I am.... I never will leave home again without you. A few days will bring me back to your arms. How happy I shall be to return to you. Life is nothing without you.[2]

Significantly, he signed it J. Jones—had he still not disclosed his true identity to her, or was this a subterfuge in case another member of her family spotted the letter? The evident affection in his letter makes it clear that Henry had no thought of abandoning Sarah and making a new legal marriage more suited to his station in life. Over the summer, he was clearly occupied with the tricky question of how to marry her legally without making her family and friends aware that the first union had been bigamous.

One problem was that Sarah was still not yet twenty-one and therefore legally underage. This meant that there was a major obstacle to remarrying validly by licence: her father's consent would be needed to the marriage. In the absence of Thomas Hoggins' consent, the law explicitly stated that the marriage would be void. But how could Henry ask Thomas for consent to marry his daughter *again*? To do so would be to admit to the invalidity of the first marriage. In a letter written to Burslem around the end of August, Henry pondered whether Thomas could be asked to sign the deed that was being drawn up to deal with the property consequences of the marriage, and whether this could be used as evidence of his consent to the marriage in order to procure a licence without him even knowing:

> To be obliged to produce witness of the father's consent from this quarter would be trusting the secret to too many. His signature to the deed may easily be done if he were to sign it before either my Uncle's or my own name were to it, for the witness's to his signing it would not then know or guess at the contents. If her father signed the deed, would that be a sufficient proof to the surrogates of his consent, without either witness's?[3]

Alternatively, Henry asked, could he marry by special licence? But did the same residential requirements apply to special licences as well as to common licences? Did you need both a licence *and* a special licence in order to marry? And if not, what information would he need to obtain one? The answers to his series of questions would hardly have been reassuring.

True, Henry's status would have entitled him to apply for a special licence—while not yet a peer, nor the son of a peer, he was still a Member of Parliament, and this brought him within the narrow list entitled to do so. But such licences were only granted after checks had been made: if officials suspected that Sarah was underage, they might well demand proof that her father had given his consent to the match. Henry would not have wanted to run this risk. So he continued to fire off questions to Burslem, to find out what other options might be available:

> Another question, suppose we both or one of us resided in some parish in London and were to be asked in church three Sundays, would there be then any obstacle to the Lady's being under age or any public consent from the father necessary? After being asked three Sundays in any Church, could I have then a special licence to be married in [Lord] Exeter's house? When you will be so good as to make me understand the above matter clearly, I will then settle the whole plan and inform you of it.

The law of the land was complicated but certain, and Burslem would have had to break it to Henry that it was not possible to have a private wedding after the public calling of banns: the marriage had to take place in the church where the banns had been called. But he would have been able to reassure Henry that if he did marry in church after banns had been called, the fact of Sarah being underage would not affect the validity of the marriage. Under the law in force at the time, the Clandestine Marriages Act of 1753, so long as Thomas Hoggins did not publicly express his *dissent* to her marriage in the same church where the banns had been published, the marriage would be good.[4] Thomas' positive *consent* would not be necessary, so long as Sarah's marriage was preceded by banns rather than by licence. Only if Thomas publicly objected, before the wedding, to Sarah's marrying Henry could their marriage be stopped. But if no objection were made, even if Thomas were simply unaware of the wedding plans, the marriage could go ahead and could not later be challenged on the basis that Thomas had not consented to it.

So Thomas' consent to Sarah's marriage could be sidestepped. When this fact was added to another legal loophole, it turned out, no doubt to Henry's relief, that the law made it really rather simple for them to marry. For while the law stated that either the bride or groom *should* be resident in the parish where they were to wed, it did not make this *necessary* for their marriage to be valid. All Henry and Sarah had to do was find a parish where they were not known, and have the banns called without Thomas getting wind of them—a relatively minor subterfuge for a man who had already married bigamously under a false name.[5]

Such a course of action was not uncommon for men and women wishing to conceal their marriage. Some couples compromised by complying with the letter rather than the spirit of the law, by establishing a residence in their intended parish of marriage for the shortest period possible. The industrialist Matthew Boulton, for example, married his late wife's sister in London, far away from those who might have forbidden the banns. He later advised a friend, the inventor and politician Richard Lovell Edgeworth, who was in a similar predicament: 'say nothing of your intentions but go quickly and snugly to Scotland or some obscure corner in London… and there take lodgings to make yourself a parishioner. When the month is expired[6] and the law fulfilled, live and be happy.'[7] The marriage of Wickham and Lydia Bennet in Jane Austen's *Pride and Prejudice* exemplifies this type of evasive—yet perfectly legal—practice. As Lydia's uncle Mr Gardiner muses upon learning of the elopement: 'It is not likely that money should be very abundant on either side; and it might strike them that they could be more economically, though less expeditiously, married in London than in Scotland.'[8] In some cases the authorities might even have been complicit in the subterfuge: in the case of *Priestley v Lamb* the husband alleged that the clerk had told him that he could satisfy the residential requirements simply by taking a lodging in the parish. The Lord Chancellor refused to believe that such advice had been given and noted that 'in any case it must have been an evasive residence, no longer than a week'[9]—evasive of the *spirit* of the law, but not the letter, and ultimately not a ground for annulling the marriage.

In fact, there are numerous examples of couples marrying against the wishes of their parents in parishes where they were unknown.[10] Some clergymen were clearly more assiduous than others in checking their credentials. The the case of *Pouget v Tomkins*,[11] in which a couple had tried to marry in a parish where they were unknown but had been refused on the ground that they were not resident there. In that case the suspicions of the priest might have been raised by the evident social differences between the parties—a wealthy lad of sixteen and his grandmother's maid. Other clergymen, by contrast, clearly did not make adequate inquiries.[12] Many couples, unsurprisingly, chose to marry surreptitiously in the anonymity afforded by London.[13]

And it was to London that Henry returned in September of 1791 to make arrangements for the wedding. Writing once again to Burslem, he noted that his letter 'comes from the Great Town where I am residing to prepare for another leap into matrimony'[14]—adding, somewhat disingenuously, that his choice 'has not been made in haste.' So it was in the small and unfashionable church of St Mildred, Bread Street, in the City of London, that the banns were called for the marriage of Henry Cecil, bachelor, to Sarah Hoggins, spinster. The original church having been destroyed in the Great Fire of London, the one in which the wedding took place had been designed by Sir Christopher Wren in the late seventeenth century.[15] On Monday, October 3rd, the Reverend John Crowther pronounced Henry and Sarah to be man and wife, in the presence of Henry's legal adviser Evan Foulkes, and Peter Spier, the church clerk, who alone had witnessed over a hundred marriages there. Sarah's signature on her second wedding certificate is smaller and neater than that which appears on her first, perhaps suggesting that there was some truth to the story that Henry had taken some efforts to have her educated.

Despite the fact that the wedding was celebrated so quietly, it was swiftly reported in the press. The following day the *Whitehall Evening Post* carried a round-up of recent weddings, noting the parentage and background of the various brides. It ended with the starkly uninformative (not to mention misspelt): 'Yesterday, Henry Cecil Esq. to Miss Higgins.'[16] Henry's letter to Burslem, written on the day of the wedding itself, was more illuminating, if hardly rhapsodical:

London. Dear Burs: the marriage ceremony is over; Mr Foulkes was present. I have chosen a young woman about 18 years old: her stature is low, her shape good, her features pleasant, her temper even and placid, her mind, as far as I can judge, strong and free from vanity, her conduct irreproachable. Her name is Sarah Hoggins, a farmer's daughter. If I can prevent her being tainted by the false insinuations of female servants and the interference of kind friends, she will be happy.[17]

chapter 9

Happy Ever After?

So Sarah knew that the man she had married—twice—was not John Jones, but Henry Cecil. But how much more did she know? The story that is usually told is that Henry did not reveal that Burghley House was to be their future home until they were actually at its gates. Some biographers have them arriving by post-chaise, others imagine a less comfortable journey in which the pair rode pillion from Great Bolas to Burghley, while yet others depict them as trudging across the countryside. The poet laureate, Alfred, Lord Tennyson, devoted several stanzas of excruciating verse to Henry and Sarah's arrival at Burghley House, depicting the happy union of the supposed landscape painter and his village maiden, and their wanderings through summer woods, and then:

> From deep thought himself he rouses
> Says to her that loves him well
> 'Let us see these handsome houses
> Where the wealthy nobles dwell.'

> Parks with oak and chestnut shady,
> Parks and order'd gardens great,
> Ancient homes of lord and lady,
> Built for pleasure and for state.

> All he shows her makes him dearer:
> Ever more she seems to gaze
> On that cottage growing nearer,
> Where they twain will spend their days.

Tennyson depicts the pair arriving at Burghley—'a mansion more majestic / Than all those she saw before'—and being bowed in by the servants before anything is said.

And, while now she wonders blindly,
Nor the meaning can divine,
Proudly turns he round and kindly,
'All of this is mine and thine.'

A later Victorian account of a 'Rustic Peeress' has Henry showing Sarah around the house: when she exclaims that it is quite a 'paradise' he asks whether she would like to live there and, upon her agreeing, says 'Then, Lady Exeter, you are mistress here'—whereupon she promptly faints from the shock.[1] Later accounts, however, depict Burghley House as the very opposite of a paradise. One has Henry and Sarah reaching the avenue leading down to the house and looking down upon 'an imposing array of turrets, domes, and smoking chimneys, looking more like a small town than a single building'—whereupon Henry declares how he and Sarah now own it all—'I am now the Earl of Exeter and you are my Countess.'[2]

Working on the assumption that this was indeed how Henry introduced Sarah to Burghley House, another more critical biographer drew a damning indictment of Henry's general character:

it would certainly have been kinder and more considerate of him if he had prepared her a little for the overwhelming change that lay before her... [but] this was not his way.... With his lazy indifference to the feelings of even his wife, it would have seemed to him quite unnecessary.[3]

Worse, this account of their arrival makes Henry sound positively sadistic:

telling her to follow him, Lord Exeter got out and stood at the step, waiting to hand his terrified Countess down and lead her between the lines of deferential servants, into their new home.[4]

While the story makes for a suitably dramatic fairy-tale ending—whether that fairy tale be Cinderella or Bluebeard—it is untrue in several respects. From a topographical point of view, the lie of the countryside around Burghley makes it unlikely that Henry and Sarah enjoyed the vista portrayed. More fundamentally, we know that Sarah's first view of Burghley House was as a visitor, not as the new countess. Since this visit was at the invitation of Henry's uncle Brownlow, any declaration by Henry that he himself was the Earl of Exeter would have been somewhat premature. And Henry's letters to Burslem show his concern for his new bride and a degree of sensitivity to the position in which she now found herself.

Henry had written on the day of his wedding of returning 'back to my retirement immediately',[5] but he and Sarah were not to enjoy rural seclusion for long. Nine days after the ceremony had taken place, Henry informed Burslem that he and Sarah had been invited to Burghley. Since this would be the first time that his uncle had met Sarah—and the first time that Sarah would see the grandeur of Burghley—Henry was understandably apprehensive, noting that 'I intend this first visit to be short, as introductory visits are not always the most pleasant.'[6]

Even poets and chroniclers have hardly overstated just how impressive Burghley House was, and still is. One contemporary wrote of the approach to the house, along a winding road, with the imagination of the traveller being teased

> through the trembling foliage, by transient and perspective views of this magnificent abode…. It opens… upon us, at last, from the North-west, with a sort of gloomy, terrific grandeur, and the variety of turrets, towers and cupolas, with which it is adorned on all sides, seem rather to bespeak the solemn decorations of a Gothic temple, than the more snug and familiar embellishments of a modern house.[7]

It is unlikely that Sarah Hoggins, born in a Shropshire cottage, could have imagined such grandeur—although residing in

Henry Cecil with his wife Sarah and daughter Sophia

London must have accustomed her to some extent—but at least she was not thrust into being mistress of it straight away.

As Henry had indicated, their first visit was to be a short one. But it went much better than he had feared it might. With palpable relief, he reported to Burslem that 'Our visit to Burghley has been infinitely more agreeable than I could have expected: the Peer is all attention to our wishes and accommodates us in our own way.'[8] Any fears that he might have had about Sarah's reception had been dispelled: 'He was pleased with my wife and carried us to Lady Eliz: Chaplin and Mr Heathcote.'[9] This, however, was clearly enough for a start, with Henry adding 'More visiting I did not wish.'

Henry and Sarah left with an open invitation to return when they wished. A couple of months later, Henry noted with great satisfaction how 'The Peer writes often and is very attentive to my wife. He observed she liked Parmesan cheese when at Burghley; so he has sent her a piece.'[10] With his own mortality in mind, especially after his recent illness, the Earl was clearly keen to secure the succession to the earldom beyond his thirty-seven-year-old nephew. As Henry commented, he 'is very anxious that she should breed'. Given that the wedding had only taken place in October, Henry's announcement to his uncle that his wishes were to be fulfilled might have seemed a trifle early. In fact, by December Sarah was already seven months pregnant. In February of the following year, 1792, just a few months after their marriage, Sarah gave birth to a daughter. Christened Sophia after her paternal grandmother, she was baptized in Great Bolas on the 27th of that month.

For the people of Great Bolas, who had witnessed the marriage of Sophia's parents nearly two years earlier, the timing of the birth would not have excited any comment. Anybody who did not know of that first marriage might well have regarded things differently. So when Henry wrote to Burslem in February he simply noted that 'My wife goes on in a very promising way.'[11] His March correspondence too made no mention of Sophia's birth. Not until July 2nd—a tactful nine months after his second wedding to Sarah—did Henry pen a short note to inform Burslem of the birth, making no mention of precisely when it had taken place:

> Dear Burslem, I have the pleasure of sending you word that Mrs C has presented me with a very nice girl and both go on well. The Peer desires it to be Christen'd Sophia.

So Henry was eager to make it look as if Sophia had been conceived only after he and Sarah had been validly married in London. But counting back nine months from the actual date of birth takes us to the summer of 1791, just as Henry's divorce bill was going through Parliament. This poses an intriguing question: at what point did Henry and Sarah actually consummate their first, bigamous marriage? If they had begun to live as man and wife and enjoy a full sexual relationship in April of 1790, why had Sarah not become pregnant before? She was clearly highly fertile, since she went on to give birth to a further three children in the following four years. One possibility is that she did become pregnant earlier, but suffered a miscarriage. Another suggestion is that there might even have been a child born who was 'somehow disposed of, perhaps farmed out to a village family.'[12] There are, however, a number of difficulties with this theory. In a small community such as Great Bolas, if Sarah had become pregnant it would have been difficult to hide the fact. And the effort of keeping it secret would have involved Henry in all sorts of difficult explanations. He would, for example, have had to explain to Sarah's family why no midwife would be attending her in her confinement. He would also have had to explain to the incumbent of Great Bolas why they did not want the child to be publicly baptised. If the child was immediately farmed out to another family they would also have had the problem of justifying why, as an apparently reasonably well-to-do newly-wed couple, they did not want to bring up the child themselves. And if they had waited until Henry succeeded to the earldom of Exeter to dispose of a child who had clearly been born illegitimate before their legal marriage, this too would have generated much suspicion—especially since, as far as the villagers of Great Bolas knew, Henry and Sarah had been married in April of 1790. Finally, given the later interest in Henry's sojourn in Great Bolas, it would seem likely that if there had been a child, there would have been some local knowledge of its existence.

Another possible explanation—and one which perhaps casts Henry in a more positive light—is that they delayed any sexual relationship until it was clear that Henry would be able to marry Sarah legally. Strategically, this would have been the wisest course. It would, after all, have been something of an embarrassment for Henry to have a child outside marriage: while it was not uncommon for aristocratic men to father illegitimate children, it was almost unheard of for them to do so with the woman they planned to marry. Having a child, had it been discovered, would also have had a disastrous impact on Henry's chances of obtaining a separation from Emma in the ecclesiastical court. Indeed, since he could not *guarantee* success in finally obtaining a divorce from Emma—as the long and tortuous process, and the numerous legal pitfalls to be avoided, have shown—there was the very strong risk that Sarah would be left as an unmarried mother, with Henry forever unable to marry her so long as Emma was alive. So there were numerous reasons for them to delay their sexual relationship. Perhaps, too, this explains the particularly loving note that Henry wrote to Sarah in August of 1791: although it would be nice to think that men would write their wives letters like this throughout marriage, it does have the ring of a man in the first flush of passion.

Whatever the truth of the matter, the new family seems to have been happy. Henry continued to report on Sophia's progress, telling Burslem how 'It is said to be very like me', with a round face and blue eyes,[13] and, in a comment that modern parents might envy, that she 'is just such a child as I wish it: healthy, lively, pretty, good tempered and sufficiently quiet.'[14]

Before long, Sarah was pregnant again. Inconveniently, the interval between the supposed date of Sophia's birth and this new pregnancy was still not quite long enough to be plausible, necessitating some further equivocation. Even more worryingly, Sarah was suffering from what Henry described as 'spasms in the womb'. The pain accompanying these was 'first removed by frequent doses of opium', but a less drastic remedy had since been found: as Henry reported, 'now in the least sensation of any of the symptoms of that disorder, the progress of it has been stopt by giving strong doses of warm brandy and water, which does not debilitate her so much afterwards as the opium used to do.'[15]

Whether it was the effect of the opium or of the brandy, or for an entirely unrelated reason, their second child was not to be as healthy as Sophia. Baby Henry was baptized in St John's church in Great Bolas on January 3rd, 1793. Tragically, like Emma's son Henry, he lived only a few months, and in May was buried in the graveyard there.

But the villagers would not have guessed that this baby had briefly been in the line of succession to an earldom. For in the village Henry was still 'John Jones': as late as April 1st we find him and Sarah signing the marriage register as witnesses to the marriage of Francis Arkinstall and Martha Rogers. Within a few months, however, their life in Great Bolas had come to an end. In July the Earl of Exeter fell sick again, and died on Boxing Day. *The Gentleman's Magazine* warmly described him as a 'sincere Christian', adding that:

> If there are such things in the world as goodness of heart and loveliness of disposition, this Nobleman possessed them in the highest degree. His excellent temper and happy frame of mind were accompanied by every social and private virtue. His benevolence was great and exemplary.[16]

Henry attended his uncle's funeral at Stamford early in the new year, and after that all pretence of being plain old 'John Jones' seems to have been laid aside. From then on, he appears in the churchwardens' and overseers' accounts of the parish as 'The Rt Hon The Earl of Exeter'.[17]

The last will and testament of the ninth Earl of Exeter—dated December 20th, 1791, after Henry's legal marriage to Sarah—left certain land in Lincolnshire and Yorkshire to his nephew Charles Chaplin, the son of his sister Elizabeth. Certain other lands were to be held on trust 'for the uses and purposes expressed in the deed for settling his mansion of Burghley upon... Henry'. With the exception of some small legacies to his servants, all of the remainder of Brownlow's personal estate was left to Henry.[18]

Meanwhile, what of Emma? Just a week after Henry married Sarah, she and William Sneyd were also united in matrimony. Their choice of venue was equally strategic: on the morning of Thursday, October 13th, 1791, they were married at Marylebone parish church by licence.[19] This was not the imposing neoclassical church that today is such a familiar landmark on the Marylebone Road, but a far more modest brick building. It was, however, one that had a large number of weddings: over 600 marriages were celebrated there that same year, and even as William and Emma exchanged their vows there was another couple waiting in the wings to tie the knot.

Emma reverted to her maiden name of Vernon when signing the register, and described herself as 'single and unmarried' rather than the more usual 'spinster'—which at least emphasised that she was now eligible to marry, even if it obscured her divorce. Given the Church of England's later hostility to divorced persons marrying in church, the fact that both Henry and Emma married for a second time in church might seem to need some explanation. The reason is very simple: at the time, the *only* means of marrying was in the

Church of England, unless one was Jewish, Quaker, or royal. Had the Church set its face against conducting the remarriages of the divorced—who were in any case a very small number—then it would have condemned them to living together unmarried, which was regarded as far worse. It was only after civil marriage was introduced in the 1830s that the Church felt able to refuse to conduct the remarriages of the divorced.

Despite the quietness of Emma and William's wedding, it still made it into the papers, being reported in *The Gentleman's Magazine* on the same page as that of Henry and Sarah (although without any allusion to the former relationship between Henry and Emma).[20] After that, Emma and William faded from public notice. We know that they were with the Edgeworths at Clifton in August of 1792, the family having settled there in order for Richard's son Lovell to be treated for consumption, the disease that had killed his sister and mother. William's health, too, was causing concern, and Emma and William subsequently travelled to the warmer climes of Lisbon to try to stave off the inevitable. But William Sneyd proved as frail as his siblings, and died near Lisbon on August 2nd, 1793. He and Emma had enjoyed less than two years of married life together.

So the end of 1793 saw Henry Cecil as the tenth Earl of Exeter,[21] about to take up his residence at Burghley House with a beautiful young wife and child. Emma, meanwhile, was a middle-aged widow and divorcée without even the option of returning to her ancestral home at Hanbury Hall.

But was it really a 'happy ever after' ending? Whether Sarah enjoyed her position as Countess of Exeter has been questioned by many later chroniclers. The grandeur of Burghley House must have been rather intimidating, to say the least. Drakard's 1815 guide to the house lists among its rooms the Great Hall, the Saloon, the Chapel, the Ball Room.... Even the more domestic rooms were opulently decorated: there was a Purple Velvet Bed Room and another in crimson velvet. One of Sarah's servants has been quoted as saying that she was 'a very unhappy woman… her husband the Earl was very fond of company, and was continually having a succession of visitors… and his wife, not having been used to nobility, was always miserable while in their company, although they treated and looked upon her as their equal.'[22] But such diffidence probably stood Sarah in good stead: the waspish writer and politician Horace Walpole, not known for his charitable comments, noted in December of 1794 that 'of the new Countess of Exeter I did hear a good account… especially of her great humility and modesty on her exaltation.'[23]

Things might easily have turned out far worse for Sarah. In the novel *Desmond*, written the year after Henry and Sarah remarried, the character Mr Bethel recounts his disastrous and short-lived marriage to a beautiful young girl who had grown up in an obscure village and had no experience or knowledge of the wider world. Captivated by 'the unaffected innocence and timidity of her manners' and her 'total unconsciousness of the beauty she so eminently possessed',[24] they marry, and he brings her to London.

> Dazzled and intoxicated by scenes of which she had till then had no idea, Louisa … entered, with extreme avidity, into the dissipation of London—and I indulged her in it, from the silly pride of shewing to the women among whom I had formerly lived, beauty which eclipsed them all. They affected to disdain the little rustic, whom they maliciously represented as being taken from among the lowest of the people. The admiration however with which she was universally received by the men, amply revenged their malignity, but, while it mortified them, it ruined me.[25]

The sad result is that Louisa ends up running away with one of her admirers and—consistently with the usual fate of adulteresses in fiction at this time—dies.

Happily, Sarah's diffidence and modesty preserved her from falling into the course of action which *Desmond* might have predicted for her. And then, on July 2nd, 1795, the long-hoped-for son was born and, unlike his predecessors, thrived. He bore the name Brownlow after his great-uncle and great-grandfather—perhaps naming a third son Henry, after the deaths of the first two, was thought to be too much.

The following year, Sarah was presented at court, and her portrait—along with Henry and Sophia—was painted by the fashionable society painter Sir Thomas Lawrence. Henry, resplendent in a red velvet suit that barely meets across his ample stomach, stands with one arm thrown protectively around Sarah's shoulders. She, holding on to a lively looking Sophia, looks straight out of the picture, her face delicate and slightly enigmatic. As one Victorian writer enthused, her face was 'so singularly pure and beautiful that it is not difficult to realize how Mr Cecil fell in love with her.'[26]

It is all too easy to read into Sarah's rather wistful face that she was in truth, as Tennyson later claimed in verse, weighed down 'With the burthen of an honour / Unto which she was not born.' It is likely, however, that Tennyson was exercising poetic licence when he wrote that:

> Fainter she grew, and ever fainter,
> As she murmur'd 'Oh, that he
> Where once more that landscape painter,
> Which did win my heart from me!'

> So she droop'd and droop'd before him,
> Fading slowly from his side;
> Three fair children first she bore him,
> Then before her time she died.

It was, it would seem, childbearing rather than not being able to bear the honour of her role that was responsible for Sarah's untimely death. Having borne three children in four years, a fourth child, another son, was born as 1796 slipped into 1797, and christened Thomas after his grandfathers.[27] Three weeks later, Sarah was dead, and on January 28th she was laid to rest in the Cecil family vault in St Martin's church in Stamford. The coffin plate recorded simply:

Sarah, Countess of Exeter, died Jan. 18, 1797, aged 24.

First Emma, and now Henry, had in turn lost the two people whose love for them had brought about their divorce.

We do not know how Henry reacted to Sarah's death, although Tennyson's version of events, written almost half a century later, is one of the most quoted verses of the poem:

Weeping, weeping late and early,
Walking up and pacing down,
Deeply mourn'd the Lord of Burleigh
Burleigh House by Stamford Town.

Whatever his private grief, Henry continued to play a public role. The year 1798 saw him appointed as one of the Deputy Lieutenants for the county of Rutland,[28] and in 1801 he was created 1st Marquess of Exeter. He also remained generous in his support for the Hoggins family. Sarah's parents had died a few years earlier, but he provided financial assistance to her young brothers. All, with his help, rose up the social scale, with one becoming a clergyman, two becoming officers in the army, and the fourth a farmer.

In 1800, Henry embarked on matrimony for a third time. His new bride was the forty-three-year-old Elizabeth Anne, the ex-wife of the Duke of Hamilton. In an era when divorce was rare, a marriage uniting two divorcees was rarer still, and one in which both parties had been responsible for instigating their divorces unheard of. The Hamiltons' residence in Scotland had meant that Elizabeth Anne had been able to take advantage of the more liberal procedure for obtaining a divorce that applied north of the border. Unlike England, Scotland had allowed divorce for either adultery or desertion since the Reformation, and it was a remedy that was

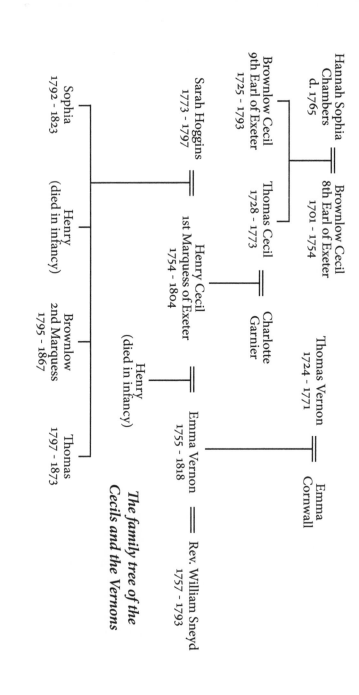

The family tree of the
Cecils and the Vernons

available from a secular court, rather than requiring an Act of Parliament. Both men and women could petition on either basis, and in the late eighteenth century wives accounted for almost half of all petitions.[29] (In England and Wales, divorce would not be available from a secular court until 1857, wives would have to prove 'aggravated adultery' until 1923, and divorce on the basis of desertion would not arrive until 1937.) Elizabeth Anne's divorce had not been motivated by the desire to marry Henry, however, having been instigated back in 1793 when he was still residing in Great Bolas as John Jones. It also appears to have been 'extremely amicable and had clearly been agreed on beforehand.'[30] But Henry's third marriage was to be his last, and his shortest. He died on May 1st, 1804, aged just fifty, and was laid to rest by Sarah's side in the family vault.

The widowed Emma, meanwhile, having returned to England from Portugal where William had died, went first to Hooley Park near Reigate[31] and then married Mr John Phillips at St James, Piccadilly, on January 28th, 1795. A few years younger than Emma, John was an Oxford graduate and a barrister. Called to the bar three years earlier, he apparently had 'every prospect which talents and assiduity could give of rising to eminence in his profession', but 'the possession of an ample fortune caused him to retire to the more calm enjoyments and not less useful life of a country gentleman.'[32] Emma and John moved to Winterdyne, a handsome house overlooking the River Severn near Bewdley in Worcestershire, where John became High Sheriff of the county.[33] Upon Henry's death, Emma was finally able to return to Hanbury Hall for the first time since her elopement with William Sneyd fifteen years earlier. The following decade saw the Phillips undertaking a significant amount of work to bring the Hanbury estates into repair.[34]

Emma eventually died in 1818, at the age of 63, and was buried at Hanbury—not in the family vault, as one might expect, but on the extreme north edge of the parish churchyard. The tombstone marking her grave notes that it is:

Sacred to the memory of Emma, daughter and heiress of Thomas Vernon, esquire, late of Hanbury Hall in this parish, and wife of John Phillips, esquire. She died 21st day of March, 1818, aged 63, and was by her own desire buried here.

Emma's grave in Hanbury churchyard.

chapter 10

Afterlives

The story of the tangled lives of Henry, Emma and Sarah is one that has attracted journalists, poets, antiquarians and historians alike—even if, as many have noted, no two writers have ever agreed on the facts. As Maria Hoggins wrote in the late nineteenth century—when adding her own halfpennyworth to the myths surrounding the case—'I have read many accounts and tales which have been published respecting this matter, but I never met with one that was accurate, nor yet two that were alike.'[1] And to add to the confusion over the facts, each generation has put their own spin on the story.

Contemporaries of Henry, Emma and Sarah, for example, used the story for their own ends. One enterprising writer addressed his series of *Letters on Love, Marriage, and Adultery* to Henry's uncle Brownlow, rather disingenuously promising that he would not 'wound your lordship's mind by minute and public references to a late event in your family, which I could trace to its general cause.'[2] Such reactions were typical of what has been dubbed the 'sex panic literature' of the 1790s.[3] The uncertainties generated by the political upheavals of the French Revolution were exacerbated by an increase in actions for criminal conversation, separation, and divorce. While to the modern eye the forty-one divorces by private Act of Parliament granted in the entirety of that decade seem miniscule, it was a significant increase on the mere twelve that had been granted in the 1780s, or even the thirty-three in the 1770s. Similarly, the number of actions for criminal conversation had almost doubled, from thirty-seven in the 1780s to seventy-three in the 1790s. And the same pattern was to be seen in actions for separation. No wonder that some commentators perceived themselves to be living in an age of moral depravity, and that pamphlets with titles such as *Thoughts on the Frequency of Divorces in Modern Times* began to circulate.[4]

Nineteenth-century writers, by contrast, focused on the romantic elements of the story. The essayist and critic William Hazlitt, writing in 1822, said that Henry's story outdid the *Arabian Nights*, and this was even before the full facts of the case emerged. In Hazlitt's version, Henry, already divorced from Emma, determines to seek out his second wife in a humbler sphere of life, meets and falls in love with Sarah, and after their marriage whisks her off in a post-chaise to Burghley House. The romance of this version clearly attracted Hazlitt more than the tragic human story:

> It is said the shock of this discovery was too much for this young creature and that she never recovered it. It was a sensation worth dying for. The world we live in was worth making, had it been only for this. Ye Thousand and One Tales of the Arabian Nights' Entertainment! hide your diminished heads! I never wish to have been a lord, but when I think of this story.[5]

Nineteenth-century writers seem to have revelled in the idea of the young, modest girl who was elevated to wealth and rank. Sarah's story was the inspiration in 1822 for *You Remember Ellen*, one of a collection of *Irish Melodies* by the poet Thomas Moore:

> You remember Ellen, our hamlet's pride,
> How meekly she bless'd her humble lot,
> When the stranger, William, had made her his bride,
> And love was the light of their lowly cot.
> Together they toil'd through winds and rains,
> Till William at length in sadness said,
> We must seek our fortune on other plains,
> Then, sighing, she left her lowly shed.
> They roam'd a long and a weary way,
> Nor much was the maiden's heart at ease,

When now, at close of one stormy day,
They see a proud castle among the trees.
To-night, said the youth, we'll shelter there;
The wind blows cold, the hour is late!
So he blew the horn with a chieftain's air,
And the porter bow'd as they pass'd the gate.
Now, welcome, Lady! Exclaim'd the youth,
This castle is thine, and these dark woods all!
She believed him crazed, but his words were truth,
For Ellen is Lady of Rosna hall!
And dearly the Lord of Rosna loves
What William the stranger wooed and wed;
And the light of bliss, in these lordly groves
Is pure as it shone in the lowly shed.

Tennyson's poem *The Lord of Burleigh*, first published in 1842, clearly owed much to *You Remember Ellen*, and kept the story alive for a new generation. Even Queen Victoria was reported to have read it, and to have wept over it.[6] A glancing reference in Elizabeth Gaskell's novel *Cranford* a decade later indicates that the story was sufficiently well known not to need further elaboration: referring to the doctor Mr Hoggins, whose name was considered coarse in refined Cranford circles, it was noted that 'We had hoped to discover a relationship between him and that Marchioness of Exeter whose name was Molly Hoggins; but the man, careless of his own interests, utterly ignored and denied any such relationship.'[7] *The Lady's Newspaper* assumed in 1860 that 'the incidents are probably familiar to almost every reader'.[8] And as late as 1898 *The Girl's Own Paper* was praising the much-quoted verse of Tennyson's that began with the phrase 'weeping, weeping late and early' as 'an admirable specimen of English trochaic verse in its most characteristic form'—not a sentence one can imagine reading in any magazine written for teenagers today!—and recommending that it be learned by heart.[9]

Sarah's story also provided inspiration for artists and performers. The Pre-Raphaelite painter John Everett Millais's

1857 picture *The Lord of Burleigh* did not depict Henry at all, but rather a wan and fading Sarah, her deathbed surrounded by tender female attendants. Some years later Millais was also responsible for arranging a series of tableaux from Tennyson's poem, organised as a fund-raising event for the Building Fund of the Soho Club and Home for Working Girls.[10] (The entry fee—either one guinea or 10/6d—presumably ensured that very few working girls could afford to attend the event themselves.[11]) We even have what one might call *Sarah Hoggins: The Musical*—in the form of a 'pastoral cantata' composed by the now rather obscure Francesco Schira.[12] Performed at Birmingham in 1875 with a libretto by the even more obscure Desmond Lumley Ryan, *The Lord of Burleigh* followed Tennyson's romantic version of the story, depicting a powerful lord, wandering around the country in search of subjects to sketch, and passing by his Christian name, wooing and wedding the beautiful rustic maiden 'Marian'—perhaps deemed a more romantic name than Sarah Hoggins—before taking her to his ancestral home and throwing off his disguise. In the best operatic traditions, Marian then suffers a decline and dies 'like a lily drooping.'[13] The reviewer in *The Times* noted that while this 'throws a gloom over the whole' it also gave the composer 'an excellent opportunity for effective climax, of which he has happily availed himself, something after the manner of one of Sir Julius Benedict's most memorable cantatas, in which St Cecilia, like poor Marian, is borne up to Heaven on angels' wings.'[14] It was apparently 'performed with great success.'[15]

The story of Henry and Sarah also became linked in the public mind with that of another fabled cross-class liaison, that of 'King Cophetua and the beggar-maid', not least because Tennyson's 1842 collection of poetry had also included a poem on this theme. King Cophetua was said to have been uninterested in women until he fell in love at first sight with a young woman begging outside his palace. In 1877, the historian of Britain's aristocracy Edward Walford, in his *Tales of our*

Great Families, has Henry invoking this precedent, vowing to choose his second wife on the basis of her virtue rather than trying to make a socially suitable match:

> 'Courts, and courtiers, and coronets,' he would say, at all events to himself, 'are all very well in their way; but… if I can only find a plain, homely and truly virtuous maiden, in whatever sphere of life I discover her, in hall, in manor-house, in parsonage, or in cottage, then I swear with King Cophetua, "This beggar-maid shall be my queen".'[16]

By the end of the nineteenth century this inevitable pairing was perhaps wearing a little thin: as one commentator drily noted, 'these delightful instances belong to the days of romance, and even then, they would seem, from the prominence given to them, to have been rather the exception than the rule.'[17] But Victorian writers knew nothing of the bigamy, and assumed that Henry had come to Great Bolas only when he was free to wed. Some combined the date of the second marriage to Sarah with the venue of the first, claiming that they had married in Great Bolas in October of 1791; others got the date right but omitted to mention that the divorce from Emma had come later. By the end of the century, however, the bigamous nature of Henry's first marriage to Sarah had come to light. An otherwise obscure writer by the name of W.O. Woodall examined the registers of Great Bolas and found the marriage to 'John Jones' recorded there in 1790. This, he pointed out, cast the key characters in a rather less sympathetic light. If Sarah knew that she was going through an empty ceremony of marriage with a man who was already legally married, then she would be no more than a mistress, and 'would show herself a very commonplace character indeed, utterly unworthy to be sung by any poet'. On the other hand, if Henry had deceived her, and kept his first marriage a secret, this 'does not make us take a very romantic view of the character of the Lord of Burleigh.'[18] The satirical magazine

Punch gleefully seized on these revelations to rewrite Tennyson's version:

> Oh! he was an artful party,
> And that marriage was a crime.
> He'd a wife alive and hearty.
> Though she'd left him for a time.[19]

Not that these findings damped the enthusiasm for the more romantic version of the story, or the tendency to use 'the Lord of Burleigh' as shorthand for one who wished to be loved for himself alone rather than for his status.[20] But for a later generation, the inequality of the relationship was to prove less attractive. In Dorothy L. Sayers' 1937 novel *Busman's Honeymoon*, Peter Wimsey's mother worries what his less wealthy bride-to-be, Harriet Vane, will be able to give him as a wedding present—'because there isn't an awful lot, really, one can give a very well-off man, unless one is frightfully well off oneself… but all the same, nobody really wants to be kindly told that they can't bring a better gift than their sweet selves—very pretty but so patronising and Lord of Burleigh.'[21]

The twentieth century saw the story again taking to the stage, this time as a ballet. Frederick Ashton's *The Lord of Burleigh* was again based on Tennyson's poem, with music by Mendelssohn, although Sarah had become 'Katie Willows' and a new twist was added by drawing on another of Tennyson's poems, *Lady Clara Vere de Vere*, and imagining that this haughty damsel had spurned the Lord of Burleigh. *The Times* praised the ballet as a 'charming divertissement' but acknowledged that it had a 'slender plot.'[22] Despite this, it was performed numerous times over the following years, and one of the dances was revived at a celebration of Ashton's career as late as 1970.[23]

The 1960s and 1970s also saw the publication of two full-length books devoted to the story. *The Lord of Burghley* and *The Cottage Countess* both devoted considerable attention to Henry's life in Great Bolas and from their pages Sarah emerges as a fully imagined character with a distinct personality of her own rather than the sweet symbol of rustic maidenhood beloved of Victorian writers. In this, of course, they were just as characteristic of their own era as Tennyson was of his.

Emma featured but little in any of these retellings. Yet she has not been forgotten either. At Hanbury Hall, one of the highlights of the guided tour today is the account of her love affair and elopement with the curate. She may not have inspired either song or dance, but her story is told through a series of charming pictures on the place settings in the dining room. And her ghost is reputed to walk the graveyard, perhaps still looking for her lost love.

Bibliography

Collections

The correspondence in letters between Henry and the Reverend Burslem and others is kept at Burghley House.

Borthwick Institute of Historical Research (BIHR).
London Metropolitan Archives (LMA).
National Archives (NA).
Parliamentary Archives (PA).
Worcester Record Office (WRO).

Newspapers

Evening Mail (*EM*)
The Englishwoman's Domestic Magazine (*EDM*)
Gazetteer & New Daily Advertiser (*G&NDA*)
General Advertiser (*GA*)
General Evening Post (*GEP*)
Gentleman's Magazine (*GM*)
The Girl's Own Paper (*GOP*)
The Lady's Magazine (*LM*)
The Lady's Newspaper (*LN*)
Lloyd's Evening Post (*LlEP*)
London Chronicle (*LC*)
London Evening Post (*LEP*)
Middlesex Journal & Evening Advertiser (*MJ&EA*)
Morning Advertiser (*MA*)
Morning Chronicle (*MC*)
Morning Chronicle & London Advertiser (*MC&LA*)
Morning Post & Daily Advertiser (*MP&DA*)
New Zealand Graphic & Ladies' Journal (*NZG&LJ*)
The Observer (*Obs*)
Oracle & Public Advertiser (*O&PA*)
Public Advertiser (*PA*)
St James's Chronicle or the British Evening Post (*SJC*)
The Star (*Star*)

Bibliography

The Sun (*Sun*)
The Times (*Times*)
Town & Country Magazine (*T&CM*)
Weekly Journal or British Gazetteer (*WJ*)
Whitehall Evening Post (*WEP*)
Woodfall's Register (*WR*)

Books, Articles and Chapters

An Account of the Origin and the Progress of the Unfortunate differences between Sir Cuthbert Shafto of Bavington and his Lady (pamphlet, 1797).

Anderson, Stuart. 'Legislative Divorce—Law for the Aristocracy?' in Rubin and Sugarman (eds), *Law, Economy and Society, 1750-1914* (London: Professional Books/Butterworths, 1984).

Andrew, Donna T. '"Adultery à-la-Mode": Privilege, the Law and Attitudes to Adultery 1770-1809' (1997) 19 *The Historical Association* 5.

Andrews, William. *Literary Byways* (Hull Press, 1898).

Austen, Jane. *Pride and Prejudice* (London: Penguin Popular Classics, 1994 (1813)); and *Emma* (London: Penguin Classics, 1985 (1816)).

Bailey, Joanne. *Unquiet Lives: Marriage and Marriage Breakdown in England, 1660–1800* (CUP, 2003).

Binhammer, Katherine. 'The Sex Panic of the 1790s' (1996) 6(3) *Journal of the History of Sexuality* 409.

Brewer, John. *A Sentimental Murder: Love and Madness in the Eighteenth Century* (London: HarperCollins, 2004).

Burney, Fanny. *Cecilia* (Oxford World Classics, 1999 (1782)).

By Authority. Ten Thousand Pounds Damages. Summer Assizes. Trial at Ennis, County of Clare, on 27th July, 1804 (pamphlet, NY: Dornin and Byrne).

Cannon, John. *Aristocratic Century* (CUP, 1984).

Cobbett, William. *Advice to Young Men* (1829).

Elderwick, David. *The Lord of Burghley and Sarah Hoggins: The true story of a Shropshire miller's daughter who became a Countess* (privately printed, 1982).

Fielding's origin, progress and present state of the peerage of England, Scotland and Ireland (London, 1783).

Fletcher, Rev. W.G.D. 'The Lord of Burleigh and Sarah Hoggins' (1913) *Notes and Queries*, 11th Series, vol. VII, February 1st; and 'The True Story of the Marriage of "The Lord of Burleigh" and Sarah Hoggins' (1914) *Transactions of the Shropshire Archaeological and Natural History Society*, 4th Series, vol. IV, p.317.

Ganev, Robin. 'Milkmaids, Ploughmen, and Sex in Eighteenth-Century Britain' (2007) 16(1) *Journal of the History of Sexuality* 40.

Gatrell, Vic. *City of Laughter: Sex and Satire in Eighteenth-Century London* (London: Atlantic Books, 2007).

Gaskell, Elizabeth. *Cranford* (OUP, 2011 (1852)).

Gervat, Claire. *Elizabeth: The Scandalous Life of the Duchess of Kingston* (Century, 2003).

Hanbury Hall and Garden (National Trust).

Harris, Andrew. *The Vernons of Hanbury: The Rise and Fall of a Landed Family* (CD book, 2009).

Hazlitt, William. 'Table Talk—No IV' (1822) IV *New Monthly Magazine* 444.

Horn, John. *A history or description, general and circumstantial, of Burghley House, the seat of the Right Honourable the Earl of Exeter* (Shrewsbury, 1797).

Inchbald, Elizabeth. *A Simple Story* (OUP, 1998 (1791)).

Inglis-Jones, Elizabeth. *The Lord of Burghley* (Faber & Faber, 1964).

Journal of the House of Lords (JHL).

Leneman, Leah. *Alienated Affections: The Scottish Experience of Divorce and Separation, 1684-1830* (Edinburgh: EUP, 1998).

Letters on Love, Marriage, and Adultery; Addressed to the Rt. Hon. The Earl of Exeter (London, 1789).

Linehan, P. (ed) *St John's College Cambridge: A History* (Woodbridge: Boydell Press, 2011).

Lloyd, Sarah. *Charity and poverty in England, c.1680-1820: Wild and visionary schemes* (Manchester: MUP, 2009).

Malcolmson, A.P.W. *The Pursuit of the Heiress: Aristocratic Marriage in Ireland 1740-1840* (Belfast: Ulster Historical Foundation, 2006).

Mavor, Elizabeth. *The Virgin Mistress: A Study in Survival* (London: Chatto & Windus, 1964).

Moore, Wendy. *How to Create the Perfect Wife: Georgian Britain's most ineligible bachelor and his quest to cultivate the ideal woman* (London: Weidenfeld & Nicholson, 2013).

Napier, George G. *The Homes and Haunts of Alfred Lord Tennyson* (Glasgow: James Maclehose & Sons, 1892).

Oxford Dictionary of National Biography (OUP, 2004)

Probert, Rebecca. *Marriage Law and Practice in the Long Eighteenth Century: A Reassessment* (CUP, 2009), ch.6.

The Remarkable Trial of the Rev. William Sneyd, for Seducing, Debauching, and Carrying Off, the wife of Henry Cecil, Esq. (pamphlet, London: 1790)

Report of the Proceedings upon an Inquisition of Damages in a Cause between the Rev. George Markham, Plaintiff, and John Fawcett, Esq., Defendant (London: Ridgway, 1802)

Russell, Gilliam. 'The Theatre of Crim. Con.: Thomas Erskine, Adultery and Radical Politics in the 1790s' in Davis and Pickering (eds), *Unrespectable Radicals: Popular Politics in the Age of Reform* (Abingdon: Ashgate, 2008).

Salopian Shreds and Patches, vols. II and X.

Sayers, Dorothy L. *Busman's Honeymoon* (London: Hodder & Stoughton, 1993 (1937)).

Shebbeare, John. *The Marriage Act* (London, 1754).

Sibbit, Adam. *Thoughts on the Frequency of Divorces in Modern Times* (London, 1800)

Smith, Charlotte. *Desmond* (Broadview, 2001 (1792)).

Staves, Susan. 'Money for Honor: Damages for Criminal Conversation' (1982) 11 *Studies in Eighteenth-Century Culture* 279.

Stebbing, Henry. *A dissertation on the power of states to deny civil protection to the marriages of minors made without the consent of their parents or guardians* (London, 1755).

Stone, Lawrence. *Road to Divorce: A History of the Making and Breaking of Marriage in England* (OUP, 1995 (1990)) (RtoD); and *Uncertain Unions & Broken Lives: Intimate and Revealing Accounts of Marriage and Divorce in England* (OUP, 1995) (UUBL).

Thomas, David. 'The Social Origins of Marriage Partners of the British Peerage in the Eighteenth and Nineteenth Centuries' (1972) 26 *Population Studies* 99.

Treachery and Adultery. 10,000l. Damages! Trial of Benjamin Boddington, Esq. for Adultery with Mrs Boddington, His Cousin's Wife; before the Sheriff of London, on Friday the 8th of September, 1797 (London: undated)

The Trial of Francis William Sykes, Esq. for Adultery with the Wife of Captain Parslow, of the Third Regiment of Dragoons (London: J. Ridgway: 3rd ed. 1789).

The Trial of John Belenden Gawler, Esq. for Adultery with Lady Valentia (London: Lewis, 1796).

The Trial of John M'Taggart, Esq. for Adultery with the Wife of Jesse Gregson, Esq. (London: 1808).

The Trial of Mr Cooke, Malt Distiller, of Stratford, for the Crime of Adultery with Mrs. Walford (London: Lewis & Symonds, 1789).

The Trial of Thomas Thomson and Lavinia Whitney, on an indictment for a conspiracy (London, 1730).

Turner, David M. *Fashioning Adultery: Gender, Sex and Civility in England, 1660-1740* (CUP, 2002).

Two Actions for Criminal Conversation, with the Whole of the Evidence, tried before the Right Hon. Lord Kenyon, in the Court of King's-Bench, Westminster-Hall, on Wednesday, June 26, 1790 (London: Smith, 1790).

Uglow, Jenny. *The Lunar Men* (London: Faber & Faber, 2002).

Vaisey, David. (ed) *The Diary of Thomas Turner, 1754-1765* (OUP, 1984).

Bibliography

Vickery, Amanda. *Behind Closed Doors: At Home in Georgian England* (New Haven: YUP, 2009).

Walford, Edward. *Tales of our Great Families* (London: Hurst & Blackett, 1877), vol. 1.

Waller, Maureen. *The English Marriage: Tales of Love, Money and Adultery* (London: John Murray, 2009).

Watson, Sydney John. *The Cottage Countess* (Allen Figgis & Co., 1974).

Woodall, W.O. 'The Lord of Burghley and Sarah Hoggins', *Notes and Queries*, 8th Series, vol. 1, May 14th, 1892.

Illustrations

Page *ii*, West elevation of Burghley House in 1755, by John Haynes, reproduced by kind permission of Burghley House.

Page 9, Brownlow Cecil, painted by Angelica Kauffman, reproduced by kind permission of Burghley House.

Page 23, St George's, Hanover Square, by T. Malton, 1787.

Page 48, Great Bolas church, © A. Holmes.

Page 108, Lord Thurlow, by George Romney, 1784.

Page 128, Henry, Sarah and Sophia, by Sir Thomas Lawrence, reproduced by kind permission of Burghley House.

Page 140, Emma's grave in Hanbury churchyard.

Acknowledgments

The authors would like to thank Jon Culverhouse, archivist at Burghley House, for sharing his invaluable knowledge of the Cecils; Andrew Harris for sharing his equally comprehensive knowledge of the Vernons; Tony Meredith, for his excellent tour of Hanbury Hall; the team at Chocolate Media, for introducing us to Henry's correspondence with Burslem; and to Julian Fellowes for a fascinating discussion of its implications.

Notes

Introduction

1 Published in CD book format.

Chapter 1

1 His wife Arabella was a niece of the eighth Countess of Exeter: 'Aufrère, George René', in *Oxford DNB*.
2 *WJ*, 25/7/1724.
3 Cannon, p.71.
4 Ibid, p.72.
5 *GEP*, 21-23/7/1723.
6 *Fielding's*, p.26. Letitia Townshend married Brownlow Cecil on 24/7/1749.
7 Inglis-Jones, p.46.
8 *GEP*, 11-13/4/1751.
9 Her surname is variously given as Garnier, Gornier and Gardner in different sources.
10 NA, RG 7/248, 20/2/1751.
11 Mavor, p.62.
12 *MA*, 13/5/1748.
13 See Probert, ch.6.
14 Cannon, p.77.
15 Stebbing, p.48.
16 Austen, *Pride and Prejudice*, ch.33.
17 Cited by Inglis-Jones, p.47.
18 Walford, p.65.
19 *LEP*, 24-26/4/1770.
20 Inglis-Jones, p.52.
21 I am grateful to Jon Culver house for this information.
22 Thomas Cecil died at Loo in 1773: *LEP*, 31/8-2/9/1773.
23 Beales, p.165.
24 *G&NDA*, 10/3/1775.
25 *MJ&EA*, 19-21/3/1776.
26 See Gervat, ch.13.
27 *Hanbury Hall*, p.15.

28 WRO, ref. 705:7/7335/73/i/2.
29 Quoted by Harris, p.90.
30 *Conran v Lowe* (1754) 161 ER 630.
31 See *Read v Passer* (1794) 170 ER 332; *Lawrence v Dixon* (1792) 170 ER 123.
32 See further Probert, ch.5.
33 *Trial of Thomas Thomson*, p.13.
34 Harris, p.90.
35 Ibid.
36 *SJC*, 14-17/12/1771.
37 Harris, p.95.
38 Ibid, p.96.
39 WRO, ref. 705:7/7335/73/i/2.
40 Burney, p.930.
41 Malcolmson, p.142.
42 Ibid.
43 Inglis-Jones, p.57.
44 Malcolmson, p.129.
45 Cannon, p.90.
46 Shebbeare, p.149
47 Thomas, tables 4 and 7.

Chapter 2

1 Letter to Burslem, 29/9/1789.
2 Quoted by Inglis-Jones, p.60.
3 *WR*, 7/6/1791.
4 *WEP*, 10-12/5/1791.
5 *Hanbury Hall*, p.15.
6 See further Harris, pp.100-102.
7 Malcolmson, p.142.
8 Quoted by Inglis-Jones, p.61.
9 Harris, p.104, Tree XI.
10 See Moore, p.127.
11 Beales, pp.189-90.
12 Austen, *Emma*, p.154.
13 Andrew, p.13.
14 *Times*, 27/3/1786.
15 See Inglis-Jones, p.68.

16 Birmingham's famous Rotunda now stands on the site.

Chapter 3

1 *Star*, 11/7/1789.
2 Harris, p.107.
3 *Shreds and Patches*, vol. X, p.163.
4 Fletcher, 'The Lord of Burleigh', p.83.
5 Ibid.
6 Watson, p.15
7 Inglis-Jones, p.17.
8 Walford, p.67.
9 Watson, p.30.
10 Cobbett, para.94.
11 Walford, p.68.
12 Ibid, p.69.
13 Ibid, pp.69-70.
14 Ibid, p.70.
15 Letter to Burslem, dated 3/9/1789.
16 *LM*, 1784, pp.322-3.
17 Lloyd, p.260.
18 Letter to Burslem, dated 14/11/1789.
19 Inglis-Jones, p.39.
20 Ibid, p.36.
21 Watson, p.50.
22 Ibid, p.51.
23 Undated song cited in Ganev.
24 *Shreds and Patches*, vol. X, p.163.
25 Ibid, 25/11/1891, p.170.
26 Woodall, p.387.
27 Ibid, p.388.
28 Thomas, p.108.

Chapter 4

1 Watson, pp.115.
2 *Shreds and Patches*, vol. X, p.143. Hodnet Heath was an area of marshy, lowland heath (presumably difficult to drive a pig across?).
3 Inglis-Jones, p.44.
4 *Times*, 16/3/1945, p.2.
5 Inglis-Jones, p.90.
6 See Vaisey, diary entry for 23/10/57.
7 *Shreds and Patches*, vol. X, p.151.
8 See Fletcher, True Story.
9 Letter to Burslem, 30/3/1790.
10 Letter to Burslem, April 1790.
11 Letter to Burslem, April 1790.
12 *Times*, 28/10/1791.
13 *WR*, 19/1/1791.
14 *LEP*, 19/1/1791.
15 *MC*, 20/1/1791.
16 Ibid, 12/2/1791.
17 See generally Probert, ch.8.
18 *Obs*, 5/10/1823, p.3.
19 *GEP*, 29/5/1790.
20 *LEP*, 15-18/9/1744; *GA*, 30/9/1746.
21 The Proceedings of the Old Bailey, 26/5/1790.
22 See e.g. *LC*, 29/3/1785.
23 The Proceedings of the Old Bailey, 6/12/1693.
24 *GEP*, 29/3/1791.
25 *WEP*, 10/7/1790.
26 *MC&LA*, 24/1/1786.
27 *Obs*, 25/7/1796, p.3.
28 Ibid, 17/4/1800, p.4. See also 4/12/1803, p.3.
29 *SJC*, 18-21/11/1775.
30 *LEP*, 7-9/8/1759.
31 Ibid, 31/5-3/6/1766.
32 Ibid, 14-17/2/1767; *LC*, 28-30/4/1767.
33 *SJC*, 1-3/11/1768.
34 *MC&LA*, 23/12/1775.

35 *G&NDA*, 30/6/1779.
36 Gatrell, p.302.
37 For an account of the divorce see Vickery, p.142
38 With occasional interruptions: see 'Thurlow, Edward, first Baron Thurlow', *Oxford DNB*.
39 Gatrell, p.322.
40 Inchbald, p.248.
41 See e.g. Brewer; Waller, p.140.
42 *An Account of the Origin and the Progress*.
43 *Obs*, 30/8/1824, p.4.
44 Letter to Burslem, 31/10/1790.

Chapter 5

1 The wording varies slightly in these pleas. Cecil's no longer exists; the language used here for both the allegation on the wife's attack and on the husband's loss is from the 1798 case of John Buller versus William Durban (LMA DL/C/564).
2 See further Staves.
3 *Report of the Proceedings*, p.5.
4 *Treachery and Ad.*, pp.5-6.
5 *GEP*, 7-9/9/1797; *Treachery and Adultery*, p.6.
6 *By Authority*, p.3.
7 *Remarkable Trial*, pp.1-2.
8 *Treachery and Adultery*, p.9.
9 Ibid, p.4.
10 *Trial of Francis William Sykes*, pp.2-3.
11 Ibid, p.10.
12 *Two Actions*, pp.3-4.
13 *Trial of John M'Taggart*, p.128.
14 See further Russell, pp.57-70.

15 *PA*, 11/12/1789.
16 *GEP*, 7-9/9/1797.
17 *Two Actions*, p.27.
18 *MP&DA*, 28/6/1790.
19 *Trial of John M'Taggart*, p.82.
20 *Two Actions*, p.30.
21 Ibid, p.28.
22 *Trial of Mr Cooke*, p.46.
23 *T&CM*, March 1791, p.101.
24 *Trial of Mr Cooke*, p.46.
25 *MC*, 26/6/1790, says that it was with a 'Lady' that Emma was to have returned—Maria Sneyd, no doubt. Edward was apparently already with his brother William.
26 The crim con pamphlet records his surname as 'Jansey', but other sources use 'Jauncey'.
27 *Two Trials*, p.11.
28 Ibid, pp.18-19.
29 Ibid, pp.19-20.
30 Ibid, p.22.
31 Ibid, pp.15-16.
32 Ibid, p.26.
33 Ibid, pp.26, 28
34 Ibid, p.28. Thompson's later became The Royal Clarence and is now called 'ABode [sic] Exeter'. It is reputed to be the first establishment in England to use the name 'hotel', and in the late eighteenth century was noted for its elegance.
35 Stone, *Road*, p.273.
36 Ibid, p.274.
37 *Trial of Mr Cooke*, p.49.
38 Ibid, p.41.
39 Ibid, p.38.
40 *O&PA*, 9/9/1797.

41 *GEP*, 7-9/9/1797.
42 *Star*, 9/9/1797.
43 *Two Trials*, p.29-30.
44 Ibid, pp.30-31.
45 See e.g. *Times*, 28/6/1790, p.3; *LC*, 26-29/6/1790.

Chapter 6
1 DL/C/0562/014.
2 DL/C/0562/015. Lushington later became a judge and was to be notable for some landmark separation cases where he granted separations for mental as well as physical cruelty: Stone, *Road*, p.205.
3 Stone, *Road*, p.185.
4 'Scott, William, Baron Stowell', *Oxford DNB*.
5 Stone, *Road*, p.204
6 Ibid, p.205.
7 Ibid, p.236.
8 Ibid, p.197-8.
9 Turner, pp.154-155.
10 BIHR, Sir Martin Stapylton c. Henrietta Maria Stapylton CPI 2256 Libel.
11 Conset, cited in Turner, p.153.
12 Turner, p.156.
13 BIHR, CPI 2486, William Parkin.
14 Turner, pp.146-151; Bailey, pp.143-9.
15 Stone, *Road*, p.186.
16 Ibid, table 9.2, p.430.
17 Ibid, p.188.
18 DL/C/181 (Microfilm X079/099), Allegations, Libel and Sentence Book 1789-1792.
19 Stone, *Road*, p.266.
20 Bailey, pp.152-4.

21 University of Durham, DDR/EJ/CCD/3/1/1789/4, Smith c. Smith. Articles 15 and 16, Libel, and Mary Whinham's deposition.
22 Some accused women still did defend themselves despite overwhelming evidence against them, for example see *Middleton v Middleton*, discussed in Stone, *Uncertain*, pp.508-9.
23 Turner, pp.148-151.
24 Turner, pp.150.
25 BIHR, Libel CPI2256.
26 BIHR, Allegation and Exhibit on the part of Mrs Stapylton, 5/7/1787 CPI2258.
27 Stone, *Road*, p.209.
28 Ibid, p.183.
29 Ibid.
30 Ibid, p.210.
31 Ibid, p.208-9.
32 Ibid, p.206-7.
33 BIHR, CPI1817, Libel, art. 6.
34 Turner, p.147.
35 Stone, *Road*, p.210.
36 Possibly the eighteenth-century Blue Ball hotel, on Coombe Street.
37 Stone, *Road*, p.221.
38 BIHR, Trans.CP. 1766/2.
39 DL/C/284, Depositions Book, March 1789 to June 1793 (Microfilm X019/149).
40 All ibid. Also William Wells deposed about the veracity of the copy of the marriage, and the copy of the final judgment in the crim con action.
41 Referred to in letters to Burslem e.g. 23/11/1790.

42 DLO/C/562/077.

Chapter 7
1   PA, HL/PO/JO/10/7/879, p.16.
2   See Anderson, p.413.
3   The language here is from the Hon. Twisleton's divorce case: *JHL* (1798), vol. XLI, p.521.
4   *JHL* (1799), vol. XLII, p.159.
5   Ibid, p.137.
6   *MC*, 23/6/1796.
7   *JHL* (1791), vol. XXXIX, p.110.
8   Ibid, p.111.
9   *Two Actions*, p.4.
10 *JHL* (1791), vol. XXXIX, p.109.
11 Anderson, p.424.
12 *Trial of John Belenden Gawler*, pp.14-15.
13 Ibid, p.14.
14 *JHL* (1783), vol. XXXVI, p.636, 4/4/1783.
15 Ibid, p.637.
16 Ibid, p.638.
17 Matthew Lewis in 1783; John Nash in 1787; and John Cope and Richard Crewe in 1801.
18 *JHL* (1791), vol. XXXIX, p.109.
19 Ibid.
20 Ibid.
21 Ibid.
22 Ibid, p.110.
23 Ibid.
24 Ibid.
25 *WEP*, 3/5/1791.
26 *EM*, 4-6/5/1791; see also *GEP* 3-5/5/1791; *Oracle*, 5/5/1791.
27 *Star*, 5/5/1791.
28 *WEP*, 23-25/4/1782.
29 *LC*, 23-25/4/1782.
30 See e.g. PA HL/PO/JO/10/7/655, p.10.
31 On this last point see Anderson, p.422.
32 At least six other wives did so from 1783-96. There may have been many others, but the survival of materials is patchy.
33 PA, HL/PO/JO/10/7/1056, 1/6/1797.
34 PA, HL/PO/JO/10/7/966, 7/4/1794.
35 Harris, p.118.
36 PA, HL/PO/JO/10/7/879.
37 *JHL* (1791), vol. XXXIX, p.106.
38 PA, Clause A, HL/PO/JO/10/7/879.
39 *WEP*, 10-12/5/1791.
40 Ibid.
41 Ibid.
42 *MP&DA*, 12/5/1791.
43 *MP&DA*, 12/5/1791.
44 *EM*, 1-3/6/1791.
45 *WR*, 3/6/1791.
46 *GEP*, 2-4/6/1791.
47 Harris, pp.117-118.
48 *MP&DA*, 7/6/1791.
49 *WR*, 7/6/1791.
50 *Star*, 7/6/1791.
51 *MP&DA*, 7/6/1791.

Chapter 8
1   Letter to Burslem, August 1791.
2   Quoted by Inglis-Jones, p.95.
3   Letter, August 1791.
4   Probert, ch.8.
5   Section 10.
6   Here the parties were marrying by licence rather than by banns.
7   Uglow, p.63.
8   Austen, *Pride and Prejudice*, p.216.

9   (1801) 31 ER 1124.

10 *Dobbyn v Corneck* (1813) 161
    ER 1090; *Meddowcroft
    v Gregory* (1816) 161 ER 717;
    Sullivan v Sullivan (1818) 161
    ER 728; *Green v Dalton* (1822)
    162 ER 101.

11 (1812) 161 ER 1056.

12 See e.g. *Nicholson v Squire*
    (1809) 33 ER 983.

13 Population according to the
    Census of 1821 (1822) PP vol.
    15, xxv.

14 Letter to Burslem, 14/9/1791.

15 This in turn was destroyed
    during the Blitz.

16 See also *World*, 4/10/1791,
    describing the bride as 'late of
    the City'

17 Letter to Burslem, 3/10/1791.

Chapter 9

1   'A Rustic Peeress', *Shreds and
    Patches*, vol. 2, p.239.

2   Watson, p.178.

3   Inglis-Jones, p.126.

4   Ibid, p.128.

5   Letter to Burslem, 3/10/1791.

6   Letter to Burslem, 12/10/1791.

7   Horn, p.14.

8   Letter to Burslem, 29/10/1791.

9   Lady Elizabeth Chaplin was
    Brownlow's sister, who
    had married John Chaplin
    on 24/11/1759. Their son
    Charles, born 30/5/1759,
    would have been
    next in line to inherit
    Burghley House had Henry
    died without issue.

10 Letter to Burslem, 12/12/1791.

11 Letter to Burslem, 2/2/1792.

12 Harris, p.118.

13 Letter to Burslem, 29/8/1792.

14 Letter to Burslem, 3/11/1792.

15 Letter to Burslem, 9/12/1792.

16 *GM*, Dec. 1793, vol. 63(6),
    p.1158.

17 Fletcher, True Story, p.347.

18 *Sun*, 24/2/1794.

19 LMA, P89/MRY1, Item 174.

20 *GM*, October 1791, Vol. 61(4),
    p.969.

21 He was formally to take the
    oaths and his seat in the
    House of Lords the
    following February: *GM*,
    April 1794, Vol. 64(4), p.331.

22 Fletcher, True Story, p.352.

23 Inglis-Jones, p.136.

24 Smith, p.63.

25 Ibid, p.64.

26 Napier, p.113.

27 *GM* has 31/12/1796 as his
    date of birth, while Fletcher
    puts it a day later, the same
    day that Thomas was baptised
    at St Martin's, Stamford.

28 *SJC*, 17-20/2/1798.

29 See Leneman, pp.1-2, 6-8.

30 Leneman, p.125.

31 Inglis-Jones, p.145.

32 Monumental inscription in
    Wootten Wawen church.

33 Fletcher, Lord of Burleigh,
    p.83.

34 See Harris, p.126 for a detailed
    account.

Chapter 10

1   *Shreds and Patches*, vol. X,
    p.170.

2   Letters on Love, p.2.

3   For discussion see e.g.

Binhammer.
4   See Sibbit.
5   Hazlitt, p.449.
6   *EDM* (undated), p.102.
7   Gaskell, p.63.
8   *LN*, 19/5/1860, p.391.
9   *GOP*, 27/8/1898, p.756.
10 *Times*, 16/2/1884.
11 *Times*, 20/3/1884.
12 *Times*, 27/8/1873, p.3.
13 Quoted in Walford, pp.80-81.
14 *Times*, 5/9/1873, p.8.
15 *Times*, 27/8/1873, p.3.
16 Walford, p.66.
17 *NZG&LJ*, 3/9/1898, p.290.
18 Woodall, p.282.
19 *Punch*, 3/10/1791, p.165.
20 See e.g. *Times*, 4/10/1875;
    5/12/1892; 27/12/1895.
21 Sayers, p.28.
22 'A Mendelssohn Ballet', *Times*,
    1/3/1932.
23 *Times*, 25/7/1770.

Lightning Source UK Ltd.
Milton Keynes UK
UKHW011809150519
342734UK00001B/3/P